WAR
ON THE
FAMILY

WAR
ON THE
FAMILY

Mothers in Prison and the Families They Leave Behind

RENNY GOLDEN

Routledge
Taylor & Francis Group
New York   London

Published in 2005 by
Routledge
Taylor & Francis Group
270 Madison Avenue
New York, NY 10016

Published in Great Britain by
Routledge
Taylor & Francis Group
2 Park Square
Milton Park, Abingdon
Oxon OX14 4RN

Printed in the United States of America on acid-free paper
10 9 8 7 6 5 4 3 2 1

International Standard Book Number-10: 0-415-94670-0 (Hardcover) 0-415-94671-9 (Softcover)
International Standard Book Number-13: 978-0-415-94670-4 (Hardcover) 978-0-415-94671-1 (Softcover)
Library of Congress Card Number 2005008802

Library of Congress Cataloging-in-Publication Data

Golden, Renny.
    War on the family : mothers in prison and the children they leave behind / Renny Golden.
        p. cm.
    Includes bibliographical references and index.
    ISBN 0-415-94670-0 (hardback : alk. paper) -- ISBN 0-415-94671-9 (pbk.: alk. paper)
    1. Prisoners' families--United States. 2. Women prisoners--United States. 3. Women prisoners--United States--Family relationships. 4. Children of women prisoners--United States. I. Title.

HV8886.U5G65 2005
362.82'95'0973--dc22   2005008802

Taylor & Francis Group
is the Academic Division of T&F Informa plc.

Visit the Taylor & Francis Web site at
http://www.taylorandfrancis.com

and the Routledge Web site at
http://www.routledge-ny.com

CONTENTS

ACKNOWLEDGMENTS

I am grateful to the mothers and children who were generous enough to share their stories with me. I will always remember their bravery and openess. The following advocates for incarcerated mothers and their children have helped me understand the hidden struggle of dispossessed families: Jonanne Archibald, Gail Smith, Diana Delgado and the staff of CLAIM (Chicago Legal Aid to Incarcerated Mothers), Mary Kay Flannigan, a Franciscan felon who spent six months in Pekin Prison, Patricia Schlosser, Kathy Nolan, Wenona Thompson of Girl Talk, Pam Thomas, Angie Vachio and Rosé Lopez of Peanut Butter and Jelly, Salme Chasnoff of Beyond Media, and Joetilda Hamilton. I want to thank friends and family who made writing suggestions that strengthened this manuscript: my sister Katy Golden, Sheila Collins, Nancy Jones, Margaret Randall, Janet Spector, and most importantly, Mary Ann Corley, for her generous support and editing without which this manuscript would not have been possible. Thanks to Judy Vaughan of Alexandria House and Jim Barnett for places to retreat and write. I especially want to thank Chris Cuomo for excellent editing advice and Mike Bickerstaff, Amanda Rice, Katy Smith, and Lizzie Mason of Routledge/Taylor & Francis for making this book a reality.

FOREWORD

I met Renny Golden at the 2003 graduation ceremony for the students of St. Leonard's Adult High School on Chicago's west side, where I had been invited to deliver the commencement address. It was a moving and humbling experience. All of the students were former prisoners who, in heart-wrenching testimonials, praised St. Leonard's as a creative learning environment run by a distinguished faculty of volunteer teachers. The students told eloquent stories of struggle, survival, and ultimately of success against the odds. The school had given them second chances to rebuild fractured lives. I learned later that Renny was one of the founders of St. Leonard's and her role in that project reflects the same kind of insightfulness and compassion that fills the pages of this book, *War on the Family: Mothers in Prison and the Children They Leave Behind.*

In *War on the Family*, Renny Golden tackles the volatile rhetoric of "family values" and turns the conservative use of the term on its head. Focusing on a group of women and children in Chicago and New Mexico whose families have been ravaged by a set of insensitive and punitive social policies, Golden is both policy analyst and storyteller. She astutely critiques the policy assault on poor families that has been waged over the last two decades, by both Democrats and Republicans, and then introduces the reader to families directly and personally impacted by those policies.

From Ronald Reagan's "get tough on crime" initiatives in the 1980s to Clinton's eradication of "welfare as we know it" in the 1990s, to both Bush administrations' pro-rich economic policies, poor people have suffered from shrinking economic opportunities, eroding social services, and longer jail terms for a growing list of offenses with mandatory minimum sentences.

In a series of interviews with formerly incarcerated women and their children, Golden paints a portrait of families and communities, mostly black and Latino, that are victims of callous laws and craven politicians but who come across as resilient and resourceful in navigating the difficult and dangerous terrain of their lives. There are no one-dimensional characters in Golden's book, and Golden does not make heroes out of her subjects. There are no perfect mothers or perfect children. People make mistakes, wrestle with demons they can't fully comprehend, and hurt themselves and others along the way. But their textured and multi-layered stories belie the stereotypes that permeate popular media. Golden introduces us to women who are victims of domestic and sexual abuse (the majority of women in prison fit this bill), and children who got caught up in drugs and violence. Still they are parents who love their children, and children fiercely loyal to imperfect parents. Simply put, they are richly textured human beings.

Golden's work builds upon the ideas of a wide and diverse range of scholars and activists including Dorothy Roberts, Christian Parenti, Ruth Behar, Paulo Freire, and Beth Richie. In critiquing the growth of the prison industry, with its insatiable urge for black and brown bodies, Golden illustrates in concrete terms the human toll that recent crime and poverty "reforms" have had on real lives. She is especially sensitive to the plight of children of incarcerated and formerly incarcerated women who have become the "collateral" victims of the system's war against poor families. For example, the families of individuals convicted of drug felonies are ineligible for federal aid, student financial aid, and other programs, which makes it even harder for them to reconstitute their lives after the trauma of a mother's imprisonment. In other words, after a woman has done her time, her family keeps on paying.

Golden weaves together an analysis in which race, prisons, and poverty are inseparable. She reminds the reader that most people in prison are poor people of color with few powerful allies and even fewer material or professional resources at their disposal. Golden suggests that the unprecedented growth of the U.S. prison empire, which has colonized tens of thousands of bodies, is directly linked to deindustrialization and the eradication of the social safety net that was forged in the Great Depression and expanded in the wake of the social movements of the

1960s. No jobs. No aid. Eroding schools, and harsh and punitive incarceration for a variety of offenses. The result is the largest prison population in history, and the majority of those locked up are people from historically oppressed racial groups.

Golden's narrative is sad and sobering, but it is not hopeless. The personal interludes that punctuate her policy critique remind the reader that where there is injustice, there is resistance, and many times, where there is defeat, there is resilience. And people resist in all kinds of ways. They petition state institutions, protest government policies, and most of all they persevere. And in several chapters of this book, Golden gives them the floor, so to speak, to tell their own stories through group interviews with the author. On a basic level, these families refuse to accept the negligible value that social workers, policymakers, and media pundits have assigned them. Golden sees this as their "refusal to be expendable, alone and without voice."

Renny Golden is a scholar-activist in the finest sense of the term. Through her years as an antiwar activist, prison teacher, and Central America solidarity activist, Golden's convictions deepened and her politics matured. Her own political and moral journey is reflected in the pages of this book. It is embedded in the way she tells the story, in the questions she poses, and in how she amplifies the voices of those it would be easier to "speak for." This book is not merely the result of a sterile academic inquiry. It is both a labor of love and a statement of political principle. The principle is that as a society we cannot afford to be vengeful and unforgiving. Moreover, it is a principle that indicts many of those in power for not simply making an error in judgment but for coldly writing off some of the most vulnerable sectors of society and deeming them expendable.

In the end, Golden, ever the optimist, urges activists to employ practical savvy and the art of imagination to find solutions to the myriad of problems facing the women and children who end up embroiled in the criminal justice system. She applauds the efforts of restorative justice programs that keep young people out of jail and give attention to the loss suffered by their victims, but she insists much more is needed. The language of restorative justice suggests the need to reinstate the conditions that existed prior to a particular crime. What Renny argues powerfully and eloquently is that the whole system needs, not to be protected or patched up, but wholly transformed. She demands that we rethink crime and punishment on a fundamental level, insisting that "poverty (too) is violence," and should be outlawed. At the same time, Golden is practical enough to know that such mammoth changes will only happen one step at a time and only through collective efforts. The addendum to the book is a resource manual, listing organizations that are taking those bold and much needed steps. The book is a tribute to them and a call to action.

Barbara Ransby
Associate Professor of African-American Studies and History
University of Illinois
Chicago, Illinois

INTRODUCTION

This book presents the voices of incarcerated mothers—those socially branded as crackheads, drunks, whores, and unfit parents. Who are these women? Who are their children? The best way to learn about who these women really are is through their own voices. These voices, so silenced and so denigrated, offer narratives that reveal the tragic, heroic, and fatalistic experience of families disrupted by a mother's incarceration. Their stories unmask the conditions of poverty, stigma, abuse, and addiction that drive women to crime, despair, and suicide. They also reveal both the mother's and children's heartbreaking and courageous struggles to stay together and to survive destabilizing conditions that are unimaginable to those whose daily safety is taken for granted. Statistics illustrating the growing number of women who are being imprisoned are shocking—almost a 400 percent increase. Social analysis of the cause of this upsurge has begun and researchers Katherine Gabel and Denise Johnston have published studies of the effects on families of the increased incarceration of mothers.[1] The demographic data about these families are essential, but like the people they represent, they are too often hidden from public awareness. These are the disposable people: women who have transgressed their social roles and the children who remain invisible—the socially forsaken few want to consider. While other scholars have addressed the dilemma of mothers who are incarcerated, there is virtually no account of the experience of their children. Further, although there are interviews with mothers, those interviews are rarely placed within the context of women's full life narratives. Without considering the life narrative of an incarcerated mother—including her own understanding of what shaped the family history that her children have endured, and what she herself lived through as a child and often reproduced—the outsider's analysis will likely be partial or objectifying. Life narratives allow women to show us the complexity of their lives.

French philosopher Michel Foucault has said that all true criticism begins with subjugated knowledge. Surely mothers who have done prison or jail time represent subjugated knowledge. Their life narratives, which describe histories of individual and social abuse, demonstrate knowledge of survival and ravaged fortitude. If we are to achieve a true understanding of the social costs of the rising trend of imprisoning mothers, we cannot simply rely on statistics, official reports, or sociological analysis. Such research should not be discounted but rather situated within the discourses of those who have experienced the effects of a shattered social bond.

BACKGROUND

My first encounter with a mother in prison took place almost twenty-five years ago. I was a new criminal justice professor at Northeastern Illinois University in Chicago, though not new to prisons. The previous year (1977), I'd been taught a great deal by the prisoners in the maximum-security wing of Walpole prison in Massachusetts. I'd been invited by the inmates to be a member of a community (Roxbury) and university (Boston University and Harvard Divinity School) "salt and pepper" team of African Americans and whites to support the inmate Prison Educational Project (PEP). The following year, when I introduced a university without walls program to women inmates at Cook County Jail in Chicago, I met Jean, who would teach me about the plight of incarcerated mothers. Jean was bright, determined, and courageous. She had the time for protracted study because she would be spending over a year awaiting trial on a drug-related murder charge. The continued hearings were the strategy of her public defender. She was a heroin addict whose boyfriend had committed the murder, but because she was present, she was charged. Further, in an attempt to get a reduced sentenced, he "ratted her out."

It was 1978, and while I assigned Jean readings on power and the elite by John Stuart Mill, she taught me about the daily struggles of incarcerated women reduced to powerlessness, and she taught me about resistance and its heavy costs. As Jean studied, the injustice of her situation became clearer, and her awareness both illuminated and deflated her. She was interrogating her powerlessness and also feeling overwhelmed by it. Mostly she talked about her three-year-old who was living with her grandmother back in Ohio. That was my first searing awakening to the constant and unremitting remorse and pain that mothers behind bars experience.

My relationship with Jean illustrates the dangers of white middle-class professional women's involvement with women of radically different cultural and social power. Jean referred to her relationship with the boyfriend who had provided her with drugs as naive, but I was the naive member of our dyad. Based on my years as an antiwar activist, teaching in the black community of Chicago's west side for ten years, I encouraged Jean to read Malcolm X, the poetry of Audre Lorde and June Jordan, and other revolutionary texts. Jean began to apply theories of power and resistance to the conditions of her confinement. As her anger increased, I tried to suggest she become strategic in her efforts to organize the women to demand changes. Already a natural leader, Jean articulated to the others the ways in which their rights were being denied. Male guards easily observed them in different stages of undress, their health care needs were attended to slowly and only if they were considered deserving by the guard and superintendent, and pregnant women delivered their babies shackled to hospital beds. There was certainly much to complain about.

The treatment the women most sought to change involved the inappropriate presence of male guards. Despite repeated meetings with the superintendent to present their concerns, with Jean as spokesperson, nothing was happening. Jean then organized a hunger boycott of the cafeteria food. That did it. The superintendent put Jean on lock-down. After days of isolation, Jean became seriously depressed, not simply because of her feelings of humiliation, the injustice of her punishment, or her sense that she'd let the other women down, but because her utter powerlessness reawakened the guilt and despair she felt in being removed from her tiny boy and the uncertainty of whether she would see him again. She wasn't eating and her affect became flat. Either out of alarm or a desire to punish Jean, the superintendent sent her to the jail hospital for a psychiatric examination.

In the hospital, Jean was drugged and strapped to a bed for two days, but in an incredible act of survival and resistance, she mustered the strategic sense to tell the jail hospital psychiatrist that she understood now how wrong her demands were and that she felt that she was more clear-headed and less of a threat to herself or the institution. Her admission worked to get her out of restraints and to be sent back to the general population and out of solitary. It also worked to awaken her sense of agency. Jean told me she'd learned a lot about strategy, tactics, and what was possible in a county jail. She was theorizing about a reality few know, least of all, the comfortable professor who paid no price for theory or practice.

Unfortunately, my relationship with Jean didn't continue because the superintendent, with little understanding of Jean's ingenuity or intelligence, thought I was responsible for the trouble and kicked me out of Cook County Jail. I wrote to Jean after that, but her case was continued for another several months, and we lost touch. I learned years later that she eventually decided to hire a lawyer of her own with the life savings of her grandfather. Unlike 90 percent of the poor, iso-lated, African-American women in Cook County Jail, Jean had grand-parents who supported her and who were willing to risk their own diminishing future to save her. It worked. She won her case and returned to Ohio where she went on to raise three sons.

She wrote to me recently. She lives in Ohio and is proud of the tall young men she has brought to a healthy and safe adulthood. She included a poem she'd written for me. I can't even say she forgave me because out of the generosity of her spirit she never blamed me for my naiveté or failure to assess the terrible price that might be paid for a theory of liberation within a system designed to obliterate rebellion, especially from women. Although Jean's agency was her own, there were few she could speak with in jail who were interested in her theo-ries about gender, racial oppression, or economic exploitation. I was the one person with whom she shared these new ideas, and neither she nor I could see the danger of my privilege, nor could she sufficiently trust her life-affirming knowledge and proficiencies when left alone in a cell for days on end.

THE CONTEXT OF MY WORK

I went back to Cook County Jail seven years ago at the invitation of Franciscan Sister Patricia Schlosser, a social worker who works with women transitioning from jail or prison to life outside. She works with the constantly revolving inmate population of women at Cook County Jail. Patricia also works with women about to leave the correctional center at Elgin and at Dwight Women's Prison. In response to her request, I sent students to work as volunteers in the jail library. Based on Patricia's assessment that many of the women in the jail were vic-tims of physical or sexual abuse, I was asked if I could interest women's studies faculty from Northeastern Illinois University in offering work-shops on domestic violence. The workshops, which have continued over the years, have recently begun to shift focus from domestic violence to the problems mothers face when they are not with their children.

I remember the shock I experienced after the first few times we showed a film—*The Framingham Eight*—to the inmates. Women in the film were beaten bloody, murdered, their fears and testimonies dismissed by both their families and the criminal justice system. While I assumed that alterations in both society's attitudes and the criminal justice system's practices had changed since the film was made at the beginning of the 1990s, the women taught me otherwise. Whenever I asked how many women in the room could identify with the women in the film, 90 percent of those tired, angry, and depressed women would shake their heads affirmatively. Then the stories would pour out—physical or sexual abuse that isolated them early and gave rise to rage or sadness and subsequent drinking or drug abuse. It was through my work with Patricia Schlosser that my first interviews with mothers and their children took place. Most of the mothers Patricia recommended had spent an average of four years in prison on drug-related charges. They had recently begun their life on the outside, struggling with the many problems of rebuilding family relationships and finding work. I intended to write about the conditions that shaped these women's lives before and after their incarceration and how those experiences affected their children. In seeking their permission to be interviewed, I told them that I considered it critical to situate my research in the context of their lived experience because I was convinced their narratives would become a testimony that both complicates and subverts stereotypes.

Another set of women interviewees came from a program I initiated to deal with one of the obstacles to both employment and a sense of confidence that the women confronted. The domestic violence workshops at Cook County Jail were very transitory and lacked a follow-up process, so they were not as effective as they might have been in addressing women's specific needs. In response, my colleague Erica Meiners and I began to assess a way to respond more concretely to the women's situation. Mothers convicted of a drug-related charge comprised 80 percent of the jail population. Many returned to the abusive or desperate situation that gave rise to their drug use or property crimes. With welfare benefits contingent upon work, they were ever more worried about the future of their families. Without high school diplomas they would continue subsistence work. By this I mean hourly work that keeps them below the poverty line—often well below. Unable to afford child care as working mothers or unaware of their eligibility for Head Start or minimal child care assistance, mothers on public assistance often leave their kids with grandmothers or unqualified day care workers. Many also leave young children with ten- or twelve-year-old siblings, although to do so is to risk losing custody to the Department of Children and Family Services (DCFS) because they are not properly supervised.

One remedy that would make these women more employable in jobs that offer more than bare survival wages is gaining a high school diploma. For example, I met with staff members at Grace House, a transitional program for women leaving prison, and learned that 80 percent of the women there had not completed high school. In response, we began St. Leonard's Adult High School in collaboration with a Dominican sister, Jean Hughes, of St. Leonard's House, a transitional center in Chicago for former male inmates. Our west side night school, which now serves women from Grace House transition center, as well as men from the St. Leonard's center, grants a high school diploma, not a GED. Studies have shown that GED students have an 80 percent attrition rate, and those who do gain the GED have minimal currency in the eyes of employers. A high school diploma, on the other hand, can change people's economic opportunities, open the door to continuing studies, and give people back spoiled honor by affirming skills, competencies, and life experiences.

In the adult high school, the pedagogy we use is an adaptation from Brazilian educator Paulo Freire's method. We begin with the participant's experience as the starting point of all knowledge. In spite of the epistemological privileging of a participant's knowledge, we still struggle with transgressing the disproportionate power relationship imbedded in our interactions. While the racial composition of the faculty is more African American than white, and thus culturally more consonant with the school's population, and while the gender composition of the faculty mirrors the participants' gender composition, the social class chasm is wide. Most of the faculty members are professors or high school teachers, and all teach in the night program without salary. The fact that faculty members are volunteering their time somehow mistakenly conveys to participants either a religious ethic, which they identify with the caring and generous nuns and staff at the transition centers, or more accurately, they may believe faculty actually want to be with them or they wouldn't volunteer. Either way, a wary trust was created.

One thing that became clear in my years of working with incarcerated women, and especially in our high school program, was the importance of family, and especially children, in enabling success after prison. Women graduates of St. Leonard Adult High School and their children were sources for my interviews for this research. I met their children at the graduations.

At one graduation ceremony, Lorraine, one of the women interviewed for this book, was nervously placing her mortarboard on her head in the basement dressing room when her three teenage daughters entered giggling, carrying helium balloons and a giant teddy bear that had a handwritten flag taped to his paw that said "Go, Mama!" Lorraine, ever the disciplinarian, turned to them, mustering both delight in their pride in her, but also a warning to respect the decorum of the graduation ceremony. "This ain't no ghetto graduation," she told them, zipping her gown decisively. The decorum was shattered during the ceremony, however, when the first graduate received her diploma. Her children shouted, clapped, and stomped, and the tumult continued with each name called, including Lorraine's.

In a world that had handed them nothing but hard knocks, Lorraine's girls and the whole assembly of sons and daughters of our graduates, saw their parent's achievement as a triumph. Lorraine's daughters had lived in foster homes while she was locked up. Their exuberance at the graduation marked the victory of a family that had been torn to shreds but had stitched itself back together against incredible odds.

Over and over again, the women's narratives contained this life-affirming spirit. If much of this research attests to the socially devastating results of state punitive policies in incarcerating mothers, it also attests to the potentially salvific quality of the mother–child relationship. In a deep sense the mothers and children "saved" each other even when their hard-won victory of reuniting as a family was undercut by the social obstacles they faced.

METHODOLOGY

In my work with the mothers and children interviewed for this book, I was confronted with both the fact of my outsider status and my authority. My relational authority in the high school was not as a scholar as much as a *principal,* a traditional term some participants used for lack of a better way to identify me. When I told them about my hope to publish a book about the plight of incarcerated mothers and their children, they were confronted with another authorial identity in our relationship—the researcher and author. My dilemma is articulated in the following, by Mechtild Hart:

> A feminist researcher who claims to be an ally of the people whose lives she studies who live in the worlds that have been pushed to the very margins by the dominant groups which she

herself is a member of, finds herself moving through methodo-
logical, ethical and political thickets.[2]

Tangled in the inequitable differences in power, privilege, and education, I sought to destabilize my position by inviting the mothers to
tell me their stories as a way to convey to others what life is like for
mothers who go to prison, and their children.

Disciplined by my experience with Jean years earlier, I intended to
listen and to contain the activist self who sought to scream at the politicians who villainized these women (mothers) in order to rationalize
their confinement. I wanted to represent the mothers' discourse as a
subversion of the policies that justified their punishment, but I was
confronted with the fact that I still had the interpretive power, and that
I could not even guarantee a representation that could authentically
give them voice. I couldn't even guarantee publication, and I told them
that their sharing—a kind of opening up of their spirits—was a gamble. There was nothing in it for them except their trust that perhaps
other women might not have to go through similar experiences if
someone could draw attention to their struggle.

Because of their willingness, and the burden of the *thicket*, I almost
quit more than once. How might this research ever benefit them? What
could I possibly deliver? When I expressed my doubts to Mabel, one of
the mothers, she insisted that I not give up. Giving up is a card that
each of the women had played, and it left their children losers and their
lives shattered. The stakes for them were high. They could not afford to
give up or walk away, and neither, they said, should I.

I have been influenced by Ruth Behar's description of the vulnerable
observer as one who comes to research not so much with an academic
agenda but as an act, however fraught with risk, of solidarity. Intentions, of course, are not enough. One's cultural ignorance can distort
the rendering of any aspect of the lives of those with vastly different
lived experiences. Nevertheless, as Behar has argued, "conversations
and interactions in the field can never again be exactly reproduced.
They are unique, irrevocable, gone before they happen, always in the
past."[3] The researcher's task is to render the stories that tell the lives of
those denied voice, "to resurrect (the moment), to communicate the
distance, which too quickly starts to feel like an abyss, between what we
saw and heard and our inability, finally, to do justice to it in our representations."[4]

In spite of the myriad ways in which I am implicated in the social
inequities that shape the lives of the economically and politically disenfranchised mothers and children I have interviewed, my political and

moral intention is to be in solidarity with those who suffer these injustices and to present their revelations as a subversion of their silenced witness. In this sense I understand their life narratives as *testimonios* in the tradition of witness literature. The *testimonio* form, used in Central America, bore witness to the hidden tortures, genocide, and insurgent resistance of peasants, organizers, and their allies. The *testimonio* informs my research.

In the late 1980s, I spent time during the war years gathering the testimonies of Salvadoran women for my book *The Hour of the Poor, the Hour of Women.* I consider the imprisonment of mothers and indirectly the caging of the spirits of their children (which far too often results in the children's own incarceration in the future), to be not only a violation of their human rights, but also a lethal form of family destruction. As in the war in El Salvador, violence, arrests, and torture terrify many into silence or despair. In the midst of so much death and destruction, each narrative is a life-affirming act, a witness that disrupts the official discourse and an act of death-defying agency. There are similarities between the testimonies of Salvadoran women and North American incarcerated mothers who have been sexually or physically tortured as children, then buffeted by social deprivations that block their every effort toward self-sufficiency and family survival.

A major difference between the *testimonios* of Salvadoran women and formerly incarcerated women in the United States is that Salvadoran peasants offered resistance narratives from within the life-affirming social power of *comunidad* (community). African-American mothers living in the corridors of poverty, social exclusion, and gang-saturated neighborhoods attempt to "cover each other's back," but the ties of community have unraveled. As William Julius Wilson has shown, the loss of black working-class jobs in steel and iron works in Chicago through deindustrialization led to decimated communities in African-American neighborhoods.

In addition to St. Leonard's Adult High School participants and Sister Patricia's contacts, I was connected with mothers through the recommendation of Joanne Archibald of Chicago Legal Advocacy for Incarcerated Mothers (CLAIM). CLAIM has been an advocate for incarcerated mothers, struggling for many years on their behalf with few resources but an unwavering commitment to defend their rights. In addition, Superintendent Joetilda Hamilton of Metro Correctional Center in Chicago recommended mothers who might be interviewed.

In an effort to understand the incarceration of mothers in a different geographic and cultural context, I spent the winter and spring of 2002 in New Mexico, where I met with mothers in another transitional facility. La Entrada de Amistad in Las Lunas, New Mexico, functions as both a drug treatment program and transitional program where mothers live with their children. Mothers on parole who need a drug rehab program sign up for the six-month program, often as a way to keep from having their parental rights terminated, but also as a commitment to rebuild their lives. This unique program is staffed by Amity, a drug rehabilitation program from California, which emphasizes community formation as the basic healing and accountability mediation instrument for women who have had to go it alone due to the isolation of poverty or addiction. The mothers share the work of mothering, the work of recovery, and the work of community building. The program is the result of the efforts of Peanut Butter and Jelly (PB&J) Family Support Services, a remarkable not-for-profit, community-based support system for the families of incarcerated parents, especially mothers.

The charismatic director of PB&J, Angie Vacchio, gave me access to the mothers at Las Lunas and also facilitated my interviews with teen mothers who had spent time in a youth correctional facility in Albuquerque. Her confidence was a surprise. Angie pointed to two books of mine in her office—books unrelated to my current research. As a result of her reading the books, her enthusiasm for my research was somehow won. One book told the story of my involvement with women in El Salvador during the war years, and the other book told the story of the Sanctuary Movement's defense of Central American refugees. Angie considered me a *persona de confianza* (a trustworthy person). Her endorsement of my efforts allowed an exchange that would otherwise have been far more guarded.

In all, I interviewed 15 women in Chicago and New Mexico. I interviewed a collective of approximately 11 children of those 15 mothers. I interviewed mothers first, then, if both mother and children agreed, I interviewed the children. More than once the mother insisted on a family interview if her children were young adults. These sessions went deeply into family wounds, always surprising me, and at times opening up space or hurts that surprised the family.

The names of most of the women and all of the children have been changed, and markers that might identify a family have been eliminated. Pam Thomas, Wenona Thompson, Diana Delgado, Martha Aragon, Nora Acosta, and Rosé Lopez chose to make public their narratives. Of the many narratives taken, I have chosen to use only some of the mothers' life narratives in their entirety and pieces from others. In other cases I've incorporated the lessons of a mother's narrative in the overall argument of the book, but I have not published direct quotes from that woman's testimony.

The twelve chapters of this book embed narratives of mothers and children in analysis. The first chapter examines the draconian drug laws of Ronald Reagan's presidency, which gave rise to an explosive increase in America's prison population, especially African-American women. The majority (70 percent) are considered unfit mothers, whereas a profile of the typical incarcerated mother reveals that most had never earned more than $6.50 an hour, 70 percent lacked a high school diploma, over half were victims of physical abuse, one-third were victims of sexual abuse, a quarter had attempted suicide, 23 percent reported mental illness, 20 percent were homeless the year before incarceration, and one in five had been a ward of the state.[5]

Chapters 2 and 3 present the narratives of Joanetta Smith and the four children she left behind who tell about the loss of their mother and a childhood of grief.

In chapter 4, the teen children of three other mothers tell poignant stories of their lives during their mother's incarceration. They reveal memories of emotional abuse at the hands of the Department of Children and Family Services during their mother's imprisonment.

Chapter 5 identifies the social purpose of the moral stigmas that inscribe the bodies of incarcerated mothers and their children. Stigma deflects public attention away from gendered racial oppression and expendability, justifies regulative policies that punish and exclude "moral transgressors," and maintains hierarchies of power and privilege. An example of policies of expendability has been welfare reform's restrictions on benefits to children and mothers with disabilities. Seventy percent of low-income single mothers with disabled children do not receive TANF (Temporary Assistance for Needy Families) welfare benefits and another 70 percent of single mothers with disabled children do not receive SSI (Supplemental Security Income) benefits. Additionally, the Welfare Reform Act (also known as the Personal Responsibility and Work Opportunity Reconciliation Act of 1996) stipulates that any felon convicted of drug-related crimes (the majority of women prisoners) cannot receive government benefits for their families. This is a lifetime ban.

These excluded families are disciplined through a carcel system (pervasive surveillance network) that is normalized. The disciplinary process flows through bureaucracies, policies, laws, and social images that prepare society to accept coercive measures as necessary for the protection of the common good. Surveillance and regulation of the *dangerous* or *helpless* people is possible through controlling images that mark them as outlaws, social cripples, or at-risk populations that need fixing. Chapter 5 includes the story of Linda and the testimony of her sons upon her release from prison.

Chapter 6 unmasks the terrorizing purposes of the imprisonment of women as spectacle, and reveals the reproduction of that terror in their children. For incarcerated women, theatrical sites of terror exist both inside and outside the walls of prisons. Women's high incidence (over 50 percent) of physical and sexual abuse prior to incarceration attests to the social terror of their lives outside of prison. Brutal prison conditions often replicate prior abuse, reinventing and reinforcing spectacles of terror within America's gulag.

Chapter 7 goes inside a youth detention center in Albuquerque, New Mexico to speak with teen mothers. Each narrative reveals a woman/ child who experienced terrorizing physical or sexual abuse and who rebelled, ending up in a detention center. They need programs that affirm their rebellion against family terror and social exclusion rather than quash it. They need, according to bell hooks, to discover their marginal position as a place of resistance, a place where their confused and rebellious instincts are not punished but understood.[6]

Chapter 8 looks at the cost to families, especially children, of their mother's incarceration. The children carry the disciplinary wounds of a carcel network whether they become homeless, hospitalized for preventable illnesses, clients of jail, detention, or zero-tolerance expulsion programs, runaways from sexual or physical abuse, or whether they are institutionalized in the child welfare system. Perhaps what is most damaging to the children of imprisoned mothers is the child's inchoate sense that the social violence layered onto their lives is the fault of their parents, their race, or their gender. The world these children inhabit is socially toxic not simply because their mother is lost to them for an average of four formative years, but because of the accumulated toxicities that surround them: poverty, family disruption, lack of decent schools, parks, health care systems, unsafe neighborhoods, abuse, violence, and the fragmentation of communal networks. The children of prisoners "read" a daily narrative, which incriminates them, rather than a narrative that incriminates the savage inequities that mark their lives.

Chapter 9 is the narrative of Pam Thomas, a poet, artist, playwright, actress, mother of two, and former felon who uses drama to construct a theater of counterterrorism. She writes and performs for those, like herself, who experienced so much violence as children it is a miracle they remained sane and lived. If abuse and terror have isolated these women, if Gulag America has branded them for life, and if their own weakness has shamed them, then their power is found precisely in that vulnerability, and in their refusal to be expendable, alone, and without voice. Pam's theater of the oppressed calls the marginal, the rebellious, and the forgotten to community. *I am a community* is a dangerous memory for the great-grandchildren of slaves, who took lash, leg irons, and loss of children, but who held to the beloved community. Pam's communal affiliation is a discourse that undermines the terror that would stigmatize and isolate them. Pam's is a theatricality that trumps the despair of individualism.

Chapter 10 examines theories of change that will affect the lives of incarcerated mothers and their children. These visions of change need to have many strategic goals: structural changes (transformation practices) and policy changes (reforms). The chapter critiques reform strategies that act to lower public scrutiny. Instead of offering remedy, the reforms reinscribe the power of governing bodies to control and coerce stigmatized populations. An example of a well-intentioned reform that expands the surveillance network is the restorative justice model.

Chapter 11 presents strategy recommendations for use until prisons are abolished and racialized structural inequities that affect the poor and marginalized, especially incarcerated mothers and their children, are transformed. While arguing for transformative strategies, I list concrete remedies recommended by advocates of incarcerated mothers.

Finally, chapter 12 presents the story of an incredible advocate for incarcerated young women, Wenona Thompson, who was on her own at age eleven after her own mother's arrest. Wenona tells the remarkable story of her passionate struggle of justice. Intense, sassy, and compassionate, Wenona has refused the master and the master's tools.

The book ends with an addendum that lists a number of transition programs for women leaving prison; advocacy organizations for children, caretakers, and incarcerated mothers; legal and policy institutes; child-friendly mother/child visitation centers and programs within prisons; family justice advocacy programs; and so forth.

1

COLLATERAL DAMAGE IN THE WAR ON DRUGS

> When we define criminal bodies, we also define ourselves. . . .
> Criminalized bodies are inevitably politicized bodies, surfaces on
> which theorists project hopes and fears, ideologies and ideals.
>
> **Nicole Hahn Rafter** [1]

Families suffer the collateral damage in America's drug wars. Since the
war on drugs began almost twenty years ago, imprisonment has
exploded. The U.S. incarceration rate rose almost 300 percent between
1980 and 1998, eclipsing both South Africa and Russia's all-time international imprisonment record.[2] We can't build prisons fast enough to
hold this war's cargo of dark-skinned prisoners. Like ghostly slave
ships, prisons float in prairies and valleys, tree-ringed rural settings
hours from the urban catchment areas.

Hidden within the war on drugs is another war whose captives are
mothers. Almost 70 percent of all incarcerated women are mothers.[3]
Their children, already part of the socially excluded, have been left with
little protection or hope. Entire families of children are cast away from
the one anchor that might have kept them afloat in the sea of social
devastation in which their lives are cast.

President Reagan's Comprehensive Crime Control Act of 1984,
aimed not at big dealers but at street-level users, cast a net that daily
fills the holding tanks of America's jails with the small fish of the drug
trade. The harsh sentencing laws of Reagan's crime bill and the Anti-
Drug Abuse Act of 1986 (especially mandatory minimum sentences)

ensured a dramatic increase in imprisonment. Christian Parenti reports: "In 1985 roughly 500,000 people were locked away in state or federal prisons; by 1990 that number had doubled; by 1998 that number had reached 1.7 million."[4] The trend continues with President George W. Bush's drug czar.

Children are destructively stigmatized by this war. Twelve-year-old Damon told me, "It was hard because I couldn't see my mama. . . . Sometimes when kids said stuff about my mama I ignored them but I didn't beat them up because I'm not a violent person." A street-smart youngster, Damon knew his mother was addicted and needed help when he was only seven, but from his point of view, nothing justified his mother's absence, his years of humiliation at school, and the loneliness and constant worry about his mother. Damon had no one to whom he could turn. Families such as Damon's remain invisible to mainstream society, and if they are mentioned, it is to vilify their "unworthy" mothers.

Michel Foucault described how the modern criminal justice system, seeking humane distance from its punitive role, hides the prison enterprise from public scrutiny. "Punishment, then, will tend to become the most hidden part of the penal process. This has several consequences: it leaves the domain of more or less everyday perception and enters that of abstract consciousness."[5] People like Damon and his mother Teena are abstractions cast into scapegoat racial stereotypes that politicians use to whip up moral outrage or fear about the scourge of drugs and crime. Their political or moral claim on a society that upholds "family values" is severed—it is as if they are disposable.

The complexity of the social effects of drug war policies on families is rarely examined. A mother's incarceration is not simply a sadness or a tragic disruption for her young children—it is a trauma as serious and as unique to each child's personality as the posttraumatic stress reactions of Vietnam war vets. Rev. Bill Webber, former president of the New York Theological School, who directed a theological studies program for Sing Sing prisoners, says that "for every mother that is incarcerated, another ten people (children, caretakers, grandparents, siblings, fathers) are directly impacted." A father's imprisonment has considerably less impact because mothers care for 90 percent of the children of incarcerated men. Only 28 percent of fathers serve as their children's caretakers when the mothers are imprisoned.[6]

For imprisoned mothers, the effects of America's gulag extends beyond their confinement within its walls. The violence inscribed on the bodies and spirits of poor mothers is reinscribed upon their children.

RACIALIZED DRUG WARS AND UNFIT MOTHERS

The percentage of women entering U.S. prisons in the last twenty years has increased almost 400 percent, while male incarceration rates increased at less than half that rate.[7] The captured are poor women of color, mostly African Americans, the majority of whom are mothers. The incarceration of African-American women in state prisons rose 828 percent between 1986 and 1991, and it continues to climb.[8]

Families targeted for disruptive and traumatic state intervention are rarely white or middle class. African-American children are nine times as likely as white children to have a parent in prison, and Latino children are three times as likely.[9] Two-thirds of incarcerated mothers have children under the age of eighteen.[10] The majority (58 percent) of the children of imprisoned parents are under the age of ten.[11] This is an increase of one-half million children since 1991.[12]

Poor families living in deindustrialized urban spaces, devoid of their traditional communities of sustenance and healing, are more and more the victims of violent stigmas that predestine their incarceration. In addition, mothers endure insinuating myths of pathological drug addiction and responsibility for the reproduction of violent subcultures. The legacy of slavery and reverberations of its image of black females as unfeminine, oversexed amazons, also help rationalize punitive social responses.

The stigmas that inscribe poor mothers are not new. Compliant poor mothers, considered the *worthy poor*, though patronized, categorized, and kept barely functional through social welfare, have not endured the assaults served upon the *unworthy poor* mother. Either too sassy, hostile, ungrateful, disassembling, or despairing, the unworthy (unfit) poor mother was punished by labels of neglect, and her children were taken by the state to be protected. In the latter part of the twentieth century, the unfit poor mother has been cut off from state welfare, criminalized, and her children cut adrift into the unruly sea of state protection or the care of relatives, themselves barely able to stay afloat. Ignored are the conditions of social exclusion, abuse, lack of decent schools, health care, and jobs that surround the lives of most incarcerated women.

The class and race chasm that separates the families of unfit mothers from mainstream culture is deep. Inundated by the media's obsession with individual sensationalist urban crime reports, the public is kept ignorant of the social inequities that confront residents of core urban areas. In a culture that lacks public consciousness of class structure, racial exclusion, and the gender burdens of poor women, these mothers and their children are both ignored and stigmatized. Their sufferings are invisible, but their failure to meet class, race, and gender standards are villainized and publicized. Implicit in the stigmatizing of incarcerated women is the supposed need to contain their violence, but the majority of incarcerated women commit nonviolent economic crimes, and their rate of violent crimes has remained virtually stable. For example, the female state and federal prison population increased 275 percent between 1980 and 1992, while violent offenses increased only 1.3 percent.[13] Of those who have committed violent offenses, three out of four committed simple assault.[14]

THE BENEFITS OF FOCUSING ATTENTION DOWNWARD

Since the war on drugs began, results have been conclusive but publicly unknown: prison construction has flourished, crime has decreased, and drugs flood into the country daily. There are some who benefit economically from these contradictory trends. An approximation of all funds spent annually on the drug war (not including incarceration costs) is $100 billion. Two-thirds of that amount is used for law enforcement.[15]

Focusing on the "dangerous classes" as the source of violence diverts public attention from crimes of the powerful. For example, the cost of corporate crime in 1997 was $338 billion, which is "10,000 times the total amount stolen in all bank robberies in the United States in 1997 and more than 20 times the total amount stolen in all thefts reported in the FBI *Uniform Crime Reports* for that year."[16] Even as U.S. corporate officers are caught stealing billions but receive minimal criminal sanctions, and as church officials negotiate away culpability by protecting serial pedophilic clerics, the cultural gaze is still focused downward on the stigmatized, who lack the legal and social power to counteract their objectification and criminalization.

PUBLIC POLICY: DISCIPLINING MOTHERS

Liberal policy makers, intending to counter the racialized stereotypes of incarcerated mothers, focus on helping women who fail their social and familial responsibilities by emphasizing the need for more social services. Conservatives want to punish unfit mothers, and well-meaning liberals seek to rehabilitate them, but either policy response diverts attention from the social inequities at the heart of the problem. Thus, the social gaze remains obsessively fixed on unfit mothers, successfully diverting notice from the lack of social opportunity that narrows life choices. These women struggle not only to survive but also to make desperate choices to protect their children. And they make these choices when, according to the human odds, they should have given up in despair.

The policy studies that obscure social inequities are informed by a social consensus about mothering that has shaped both child welfare and social welfare policy throughout U.S. history. Women are held solely responsible for children. If her crime is neglect of her children because of drug use, she enters the realm of the monstrous. The image of the failed mother is both racialized and class specific. Women are portrayed as hopeless addicts, and willing prostitutes who live in filthy conditions, wantonly choosing to abandon their children. In summary, they are viewed as women who have lost their maternal instinct.

Middle-class white women who fail their maternal responsibilities through illegal activities avoid incarceration because they can both afford legal protection and present to legal authorities assurances that they can and will seek psychological help so as to resume family responsibilities. If whites are imprisoned, they are granted the first shots at drug treatment, which often ensures parole and helps people avoid returning to prison: "A California study showed that two-thirds of drug treatment slots went to whites despite the fact that 70 percent of inmates sentenced for drug sentences were African American."[17]

WHO ARE INCARCERATED MOTHERS?

In the month prior to their arrest, 50 percent of the mothers in a California study were unemployed, and 70 percent lacked a high school diploma.[18] Steve Donzinger reports that "two-thirds of the women in prison are minorities, about half ran away from home as youths, a quarter had attempted suicide, and a sizable number had serious drug problems. Over half had been victimized by physical abuse and a third reported sexual abuse. Most had never earned more than $6.50 an hour."[19]

These are women who almost never caught a break, women who lacked the economic or social power to overcome their circumstances, women who experienced trauma as youths and then gave up or gave in. Almost 20 percent were homeless the year before their incarceration, and 23 percent of the mothers reported mental illness.[20]

The majority of these mothers came from a single-parent home in which at least one family member had been incarcerated. One in five grew up as a ward of the state. One in three had made suicide attempts.[21] Six out of ten women in state prisons have experienced sexual or physical abuse at some time in their past.[22]

The effects of violence on the lives of incarcerated women cannot be overemphasized. Two recent studies indicate that posttraumatic stress disorder can increase cravings for drugs. In children, repeated sexual abuse, like repeated drug abuse, changes in a particular area of the brain. According to researcher Carl Anderson, who conducted a study at McLean Hospital in Belmont, Massachusetts: "Damage to this area of the brain may cause an individual to be particularly irritable, and to seek external means, such as drugs or alcohol to quell this irritability.[23] Psychiatry professor Scott Coffey, reflecting on a study conducted at the Institute of Psychiatry at the University of South Carolina, said, "From our research with trauma victims, we know that intrusive trauma memories . . . induced negative emotions that increase cravings in substance abusers with post traumatic stress disorder.[24]

Even these findings, cast within a scientific framework, can reinforce stereotypes of women as pathological, out-of-control addicts. Indeed, drug relapse is common, as is women's reincarceration for illegal drug use, but the focus remains upon the mother's psychological makeup, and not the unrelenting social obstacles she faces due to a lack of opportunities to receive a living wage, child care, decent housing, health care, decent schools for her children, and access to drug rehab programs.

The effects of cuts in social spending for the last twenty years has directly affected children from poor families with a female head of household. Families with children are the fastest growing segment of the homeless population in Chicago, and they were 40 percent of the 400,000 nationwide homeless in 1996.[25] A housing crisis begun with President Reagan's 75 percent cut in the low income housing budget, as well as President Clinton's "end of welfare as we know it," has led to an explosion in the homeless population. Nearly 15 million children are eligible for child care assistance, but only 12 percent receive help.[26] "Sixty-five percent of mothers with children under the age of six, and 78 percent of mothers with children ages six to 13 are in the labor force."[27] A single mother working full time earning a minimum wage, which is the typical wage of the working poor, cannot rise above the federal poverty level. The Children's Defense Fund found that nearly 58 percent of the working poor had family earnings below the poverty line, with 50 percent of those working parents unable to pay rent, or buy food, or afford essential medical care.[28] Since the Welfare Reform Act's inception, thousands of poor people have also lost Medicaid benefits.[29]

Without exception, the families in this research have been affected by these trends. One mother shamefully described sleeping in an abandoned building at one of her lowest periods. With rare exceptions, the mothers struggled to support their families through low-paying jobs, while constantly worrying that their lights could be cut because they couldn't pay the bills or rent. They dreamed of housing in safer neighborhoods. All the mothers earned wages below the poverty line following release from prison.

DAMON'S DREAM

Damon's mother Teena lived in the corridors of desperation described in the statistics above. Drugs became her way out. Released from prison, she now fights for her family's life within a system that values accumulation over the unremunerative social value of relational mother work. Damon's dream came true when his mother came home, but he told me of the nightmares he had when Teena was locked up. "I never gave up hope," he said. He's sure that he was instrumental not simply in his mother's release, but also in her recovery from drugs. "I think the fact that I was suffering and worrying about her gave her the strength to turn her life around . . . that, and God."

The power of a little boy's love to call his mother to save herself, though deeply inspiring, is not the sole point of this book. The story of Joanetta, another successful mother, does not simply show how the human spirit can triumph over overwhelming circumstances. The other critical point is to shift attention to the penalizing circumstances—to interrogate the policies, practices, and structures that create and maintain such limiting circumstances.

2

JOANETTA'S WORLD

> Women in prison comprise an enormous, invisible and silenced population.
>
> **Kum-Kum Bhavani and Angela Davis**[1]

This chapter presents the narrative of Joanetta Smith, a mother of five who spent four years in prison on drug charges. Joanetta's five grown children tell their stories in chapter 3.

The following narratives are interrogations of power. They reveal a family that deserved not help but a chance—in a word, justice. As Nancy Campbell writes, "Women who use illicit drugs do not need pity, compassion, life skills or social services designed to help them better adjust to the worlds they inhabit. They need different worlds to inhabit."[2] The following is Joanetta's description of the world she inhabited as a child.

My mother had 12 children in all. My father left Mama when I was 13. I think we were middle-class because we always had breakfast, lunch, and dinner. My dad worked construction, but when he left we ate a lot of pinto beans. My mama was a gambler, addicted to it. She went to the racetrack to supplement her welfare check. If she lost at the track, we had popcorn or nothing.

Joanetta's apartment on Chicago's west side faces east toward Lake Michigan and downtown. From her window, you can see the blue silhouette of the city's skyline glinting in the morning sun. An elevated train can carry you to the Loop in twenty minutes, yet the chasm separating North Lawndale's people from the gaze of the people in those towers is as vast as the Grand Canyon. Joanetta's small two-flat house catches January sunlight unimpeded by buildings. North Lawndale has clusters of buildings, then long stretches of vacant spaces strewn with rusted debris. Whole blocks, where buildings once stood, lie cratered out as if an explosion erased them. Storefront churches, gas stations, an occasional neighborhood store, drug houses, and liquor stores are scattered along Roosevelt Road. So much has been abandoned here. Like a battered woman, North Lawndale keeps holding onto her family, even as she faces more blows.

Joanetta's family story is situated in the context of a section of Chicago (the west side) that loses jobs year after year as the process of deindustrialization expands, and where the school system graduates only 50 percent of its high school students. This occurs within a city suffering from tax flight to the suburbs; a city where the homeless population is over 80,000, and where the local criminal justice system targets young African-American men. The story of Joanetta and her children is situated in the context of a U.S. culture in which one out of three women reports an experience of some form of sexual abuse.[3]

Joanetta and her children left Lawndale for Waukegan, Illinois twice, but both times the family returned to Chicago and saw their return as a triumph. Now their mother has returned from four years in prison, as a recovered addict whose faith in God is so intense that it sometimes aggravates her children, although no one in her family would question the rope of light their mother grabbed in a prison cell. They dare not question the source of their mother's strength because they recognize deliverance and are grateful.

Since her release over a year ago, Joanetta has worked two jobs and bought a two-flat building that she owns with her oldest daughter, Leona. She is active in her church, baby-sits her grandchildren, and attends a grief support group to deal with her sorrow and confusion concerning the accidental murder of her second oldest son, Jackie, who was killed while she was in prison. Joanetta taught Leona how to apply for, and set up, a mortgage, and how to hire rehabbers to convert their old building into a place of pride. The apartment building seems a triumph to this family, a sign that their lives have become stable and trustworthy again. Her daughters' three toddlers and two infants are another sign of their new hopes. Perhaps their fondest hope lies with Alvin, Joanetta's youngest son. His gold and silver trophies for baseball and basketball sit prominently on a table crowded with sports and academic awards.

Joanetta's narrative makes evident not only one woman's story, but also the story of a family embedded within various systems and their struggle to resist their destruction as a family. Joanetta and her children are not a poster family for triumph over the demon of drugs. Presenting a narrative of triumph of a family that had rejected the stigmas they confront daily could legitimize the dominant culture's facile assumption that personal choice and individual moral character, rather than social opportunity, is what enables positive transformation. Instead, this is a tale of one family's struggle to survive against incredible odds. More than just survival, in a culture that holds women like Joanetta responsible for moral failure, social decay, and reproduction of a criminal class, this family's fragile but insistent practice of support for each other and desire for a better life is an act of resistance.

The social context of this family's narrative includes the social exclusion of poor people of color, and violence against women. *Social exclusion* describes a lack of political voice and economic opportunity that could raise one's family above the poverty line, and lack of resources to legally purchase protections from exclusionary institutions like the police, the schools, or family welfare. For example, between 1991 and 2000, 98 percent of job growth in the Chicago metropolitan area took place in the predominantly white suburbs and not in the city, which houses two-thirds of the area's African Americans. North Lawndale, which is 99 percent African American, lost nearly 3,000 jobs between 1991 and 2000.[4] Every one of the predominantly black neighborhoods in Chicago has double-digit unemployment, with twelve neighborhoods having a 20 percent unemployment rate.[5] In Joanetta's North Lawndale neighborhood, 27 percent of the labor force is unemployed and 27 percent of single-parent families live below the government's poverty line.[6]

PUBLIC POLICY REFORMS

Joanetta's family's story is also located in the context of public policy "reforms" that reproduce white, middle-class, and male privilege by diverting attention away from social inequality through policies and laws that target families like Joanetta's as the source of danger and moral failure.

Mainstream social theorists, both liberal and conservative, such as the drafters of the 1996 Welfare Reform Act, rationalize these social policies by using narratives such as Joanetta's to reinforce theories of personal pathology or moral failure. As the reauthorization period for the Welfare Reform Act drew near, conservative policy makers produced studies "proving" that two-parent, heterosexual marriages promote not simply stable family life, good citizenship, and moral inspiration, but also help avoid poverty. States such as West Virginia, Oklahoma, and Arizona have implemented monetary rewards to welfare moms who marry.[7] President Bush nationalized this policy "remedy" when Congress reauthorized the federal welfare bill in 2002.

The focus of policy makers is on individuals, whether it is the conservatives' blaming of poor people for their plight, or the liberals' desire for damage control so that the burden on the poor will be less catastrophic. Their solutions are either punitive conservative "reforms" or liberal reforms that make dispossession and social exclusion less cruel. There are no policies that address fundamental social inequality and lack of job opportunities that pay a living wage. As Collins and Goldberg write, "A case in point is Senator Daniel Moynihan, once a liberal and later a neo-conservative. While pinpointing black male unemployment as a problem underlying the economic dependency of black women, Moynihan has never put forth a program for job creation or full employment."[8]

The texts of Joanetta's family are documents that reveal the social costs of these policies and that repudiate the venal interpretation of individual pathology. The focus of social justice theorists is on structures that reproduce poverty and unprecedented wealth. From that perspective, Joanetta's family narrative is a discourse of resistance and a refusal of annihilation.

JOANETTA'S NARRATIVE

While her children and grandchildren are gathering, Joanetta sits me down in the front room and reflects on her early "middle-class" life. Joanetta signals to her daughter to hold her grandbaby, then she looks out the window and recalls her teen years.

When I was a teenager my mother met my second father, an alcoholic. He gave us a better life but he beat her and had other women. She went back to gambling. But then the sheriff came and evicted us because she couldn't pay the rent. She'd had five kids by my second father. We were on our own and we had almost no food.

I lived with my friend's families. I was pregnant at fifteen with Ringer. I was a virgin but I got pregnant fast.

My mother had met another man, turned her life around, went to school and became a certified nursing assistant. Then we all moved back with her—all thirteen of us. But then she met another guy and left us for him.

By then I was pregnant with Leona and I lived in my mother-in-law's basement. After I had the baby I wanted to move because the basement wasn't clean. Also, Darnell's family, who were preachers, didn't accept me because I had no high school diploma, already had children, and I was on welfare.

Then the good years. Darnell worked at Commonwealth Edison. We had our own apartment. I was learning how to be a mother, not like my mother. I thought I was supposed to be a housewife. I volunteered at school; I read stories to my kids; we did crafts together. I never asked what I wanted from life. We had a normal life. Dinner always at 6 P.M. We went to movies or to his mother's. Darnell told me how life was to be. I didn't have the guidance of a mother.

Darnell had friends who sold drugs but I didn't know it. His best friend told him he could make money selling. Darnell was working pretty hard to support us so he went for the extra money. Then beside selling, he started using.

I was real straight as a teen. I didn't have friends. When I did have friends I was ashamed. Also I was a follower. When my friends smoked reefer, I followed but I stopped. When I had my kids I didn't drink or smoke.

But all my siblings except three used drugs—heroin or cocaine. That, and the pressure for me was my mama's gambling and Darnell's *molding* me. Whatever Darnell told me, I believed him, because Darnell was decent and good. No one taught me the value of life.

When Darnell got into drugs I had only enough money for groceries. He was getting high but I didn't know it. They bagged it in the basement where he stayed for hours. Eventually he showed me how to smoke crack cocaine.

We were both addicted. I stopped volunteering at school, stopped giving the kids parties. Ringer was twelve when he looked through a peephole and saw his mother and father doing drugs. No one was there for my kids. My mother was off gambling. When Darnell's family saw the drug paraphernalia they preached at us. They blamed me for his addiction.

Everything was terrible. Darnell had cheated on me and had a baby with someone else. I took the children to stay with a friend who I had baby-sat for. When she saw I was on drugs, she told me to get it together, but she'd give me money I'd use for drugs.

I had nothing going for me. Darnell said, "You'll never get another man." We couldn't take care of our kids because we were always high. I moved to Waukegan, Illinois, where my mother and brothers and sisters lived. But when I arrived all my brothers were high. I got clean for a while but relapsed.

Their Daddy, who was addicted, but still working in Chicago, came to visit the kids. My brothers were dealing heroin so I tried it. Then Darnell tried it.

Somehow I went to nursing school. It was because of my friend's guidance. I thought I couldn't do anything—I didn't even know how to do the paperwork for the test. She did it for me, God forgive me, and that's how I got my nursing degree (LPN). She had a husband on drugs but she was strong. I wanted to be like her, to have her strength. I was still a follower.

I got my first job for $4.20 an hour and I was still on heroin. I'd known Jeff for years. I was so lonely I went with him. He comforted me but he was on drugs and he was thuggish. He'd stick up people, deal drugs. He kept me supplied. By then I spent no time with my kids. My friend watched them while I was out getting high. Then Jeff went to prison. I continued work, drugged up a lot, not attending my kids but I paid the rent. My friend continued to care for the kids. But my brothers turned her house into a drug house. She married one of my brothers and eventually the landlord made us all leave because of the chaos.

We moved to Waukegan again. Then my children and I ended up in a shelter for a month. Finally, Jeff, who was in and out of prison, got out and managed to get money for a down payment on an apartment in Chicago. My son Ringer had learned to deal drugs. By then I had chosen drugs over everything. I couldn't pay rent or for food. They were calling DCFS on us, but Darnell's mother said she would take them on the condition that I would give her legal guardianship. I did.

Then I really went down . . . lost my job. I went on the street corner with my cousin selling drugs. I started going to jail. My two girls were teens and I was afraid my mother-in-law would give them to DCFS. I managed to get my girls back, but we stayed in a raggedy hotel room for one year.

Joanetta's own childhood of abandonment by a father who beat her mother, and a mother who supported thirteen children by supplementing her welfare check through gambling, left Joanetta "ashamed" as a teen. It left her siblings ashamed also. Yet underlying their family dysfunctionality is a structural disparity that "shames" too. The expulsion rate in Chicago's schools escalated 1,100 percent between 1996 and 2001.[9] The Center for Labor Market Studies at Northeastern University found that Chicago was "home to nearly 60,000 'disconnected' [out of school and work] 20–24 year olds, equivalent to nearly one in four of the city's young adults."[10]

Although young African-American, Latino, and Arab-American men are held responsible for violence, the city commits less than 2 percent of its budget to youth support services, and federal and state summer employment monies have been drastically cut. The prison population in Illinois has grown 60 percent since 1990, and more than 60 percent of the male prison population is African American.[11] Where were Joanetta's brothers going to work, most of whom were dropouts or "push-outs"? Their most immediate option for survival was to engage in drug selling, which is controlled by gangs. Eventually her brothers became addicts.

Certainly Joanetta saw her family of origin as dysfunctional—a dysfunctionality her own children experienced when their mother and father were drug addicts. Joanetta seems to understand dysfunctionality from both the dominant culture's "pathological" interpretation and her own subversive understanding that addiction, not her own love and care for her children, was the disruptive factor leading to dysfunctionality. According to researcher Nancy Campbell, "dysfunctional families may be seen as an outcome of social practices, or as the sum of pathological individuals within them. As a nation we prefer the latter explanation, locating 'problematic mothering' as the source of our dysfunctionalities."[12]

Although utterly marginal to mainstream culture, Joanetta sought to live up to the gender and class standards of mainstream culture. Her sense of worth as a wife and mother were tied to the security and safety of a family life she could not achieve. Joanetta understood her childhood as "middle class" because they ate three meals a day. In the United States people consider themselves middle class if they make between $20,000 and $200,000 annually. According to Joanetta, her mother barely made $6,000 a year in income through both welfare and gambling, and she had to support a family of thirteen, sometimes with a male partner, but often not. Like so many Americans, Joanetta's misunderstanding of the role of class prevents her from having a collective sense of her oppression. Because there is no political entity that might channel consciousness of oppression, she internalizes negative beliefs about herself.

Joanetta has further internalized standards of motherhood and being a "good" wife. Once she was addicted, Joanetta's dream of a family life that could protect her children from the life of poverty and desperation she knew as a child was destroyed. In spite of social exclusion that traps impoverished African Americans, poor black mothers, especially those who have experienced abuse, seek an elusive middle-class respectability for their families.[13] Joanetta's sense of identity was tied to Darnell's "molding" her. When Darnell, who was "decent and good," showed her how to smoke crack, she went along. At that point Joanetta saw herself through society's eyes—a failure as a mother and wife. She internalized the stigma, just as she internalized middle-class notions of family life.

Though they are no longer together, there is no point at which Joanetta is willing to blame Darnell for her choices or for the effects of his molding her. Her understanding of the cultural disrespect heaped upon black men ensures her loyalty to and solidarity with Darnell. Whatever Darnell's failings or his infidelity, Joanetta clings to the traditional gender roles that she hoped would give their family the cohesion and respect that the dominant culture promised would be theirs. Joanetta's sympathy for Darnell is based on her knowing how hard he worked for their family including trying to make extra money through the informal drug economy. Darnell, like Joanetta, is a recovering addict and former felon. Joanetta, the shy follower who trusted Darnell's male leadership, still respects him because he has remained close to his children and because he was a model prisoner.

STIGMATIZING BLACK MOTHERS

Although her children were born before her addiction began, Joanetta was swept into the social net that sought to catch the invidious addict mothers responsible for the crack baby epidemic of the 1980s and 1990s. Legal scholar Dorothy Roberts argues that punitive control of black mothers' reproductive life is a heritage of slavery, which sought her reproduction of a labor force, and sold her children off to serve those interests.[14] The *crack epidemic* discourse about degenerate, licentious, undisciplined crackhead mothers uses similar justifications for policies that ignore the conditions that socially enslave poor black women like Joanetta, and focus instead on punishing the denigrated mother for her failure to meet white middle-class standards of mothering.

The social bureaucratic enforcers of these standards exact enormous costs on those who transgress class and race standards of maternal integrity. Poor women of color can lose their babies or end up in prison. Regardless of equal rates of drug abuse during pregnancy, black women are ten times more likely to be reported to child welfare agencies for prenatal harm to their unborn children than white women.[15]

Dorothy Roberts reports that, "between 1985 and 1995 at least, two hundred women in 30 states were charged with maternal drug abuse."[16] Initial studies parlayed by the media told the public, prosecutors, and policy makers about the irreparable brain damage to fetuses, to crack babies, and to future cohorts of incorrigible "crack" youngsters when they entered school. Policy was driven by the belief that increased prosecution of their heinous mothers was a protection for their children, but sympathy for children was subordinated to the fear of the social costs for them that would be borne by society. Permanently damaged and abandoned by their mothers, they would require costly hospital care, inundate the foster care system, overwhelm the public schools with their special needs, and ultimately prey upon the rest of society as criminals and welfare recipients.[17] The children of incarcerated mothers also became criminalized. Like their mother's pathological maternal incapacity, the children of drug-using black mothers are marked for future deviancy.

In recent years, studies indicate that the harm to babies born with cocaine in their system is minimal and results in some growth deficits that are usually outgrown.[18] These facts have done little to transform the policies that punish mothers who use drugs, especially pregnant users, by incarcerating them for drug-related nonviolent crimes, or by placing their children in foster care and terminating their parental rights to the child.

Joanetta was lucky because she began drugs after her children were born and her sister and grandmother took her children. Still, the children pretty much depended on each other, and especially their older sister, to take care of them. Joanetta struggles each day to confront her stigmatization, not only before the dominant culture that demonizes her, but also in her own mind. She struggles to show her children her strength and goodness because they too have internalized the images that portray their family as depraved and socially damaged.

Her children have their own story to tell. Their narrative follows in the next chapter.

3

LOST CHILDHOOD: A FAMILY NARRATIVE

In both arenas, reproductive rights and drugs, calls for prohibi-
tion and punishment are often justified by the claim that such
punitive approaches are necessary to save the children.

Lynn Paltrow[1]

Joanetta wanted her grown children to take part in the interview. She
wanted to place the story of her journey in the context of her family,
even when she knew her children's accounts of a childhood with an
addicted mother were painful and terribly sad. The family dialogue
became intense, not so much because of Joanetta's downfall but
because of the continuing grief about their brother Jackie's death and
their anxiety about their troubled brother, Ringer.

The dialogue below shows both the collective struggle of children to
remain a family and somehow to be instrumental in their mother's
recovery. This is not because of a middle-class version of transformed
family behavior, but because they would not give up on each other or
their parents. Reciprocally, their mother has returned to them, determined to be there for them in spite of her previous abandonment. It is
not prison or the state that has rescued this family—it is Joanetta and
her children themselves. But can they rescue themselves from the social
inequities that press down upon them?

As we talked, each of Joanetta's children reacted to her descriptions
of addiction and imprisonment in different and unpredictable ways.
This narrative reveals their thwarted hopes. It also reveals their pluck

and ingenuity. If Joanetta is held responsible for the family's burdens, she should also be held responsible for the family's fortitude. Larger social responsibilities for racism, social exclusion, and lack of opportunity underlie these discourses, but the family takes these social inequities in stride, as if they were dealt a "bad" hand and the only thing they can do is bluff and hope for the best.

While Joanetta unflinchingly described the life journey that led up to her imprisonment, her children sat listening. She wanted them to hear it so that the streets, with their lure of money and the dealer's quick escape from the blues, wouldn't claim them, especially Ringer. When she finished her story she called her grown children to sit around a dinner table. She knew that the conversation would be about her years of addiction and she was ready. Her children, two of them with infants, rarely left the table except to bring their toddler's toys. It was Sunday morning and they talked until the sun cast dark shadows in the room.

Jeff, Joanetta's sometimes partner, took care of the children for much of the day, but he was not part of the conversation. A tall, handsome man, younger than Joanetta, Jeff was very attentive to the children for about three hours, then he began to nod off from drugs. By then Alisha's partner Darren, a bright wiry young construction worker, came in and took over child care.

LOST CHILDHOODS

In the text that follows, Alisha, Alvin, Leona, and Ringer reflect on their early years. Alisha, Joanetta's second-oldest girl, has an infant and a toddler. She is beautiful, expressive, very serious. Her youngest brother Alvin, who is an honor student at a college prep high school in Chicago, was the class valedictorian in eighth grade. He scored the highest in his grade school on both the Iowa and the Stanford tests. He is an athletic star who is being scouted for baseball by the University of Arkansas and Northern Illinois University. He is the most playful of the family.

Leona, the oldest girl, is the one who held things together, probably skipping much of her own childhood. She lost all her hair to the disease alopecia at the time that her older brother Ringer was initiated into a gang at age thirteen. She is a single parent of three and she's in her twenties. Leona, like her mother, is adamantly against drugs or alcohol of any kind. She has a no nonsense approach in confronting her brother Ringer about this. She holds her smiling, fat-cheeked baby on her lap.

Joanetta's oldest son Ringer, who is soft-spoken, hangs back and listens. Ringer is slight but apparently powerful. He has two children, but doesn't live with them. He seems sad and though he has been a gang member, his demeanor is not tough. He is polite, even timid.

Alisha	I was 16 when my mama went to prison for over a year. I had a four-day-old daughter. I dropped out of school and started smoking weed. I was glad she went to prison because she was going back and forth to jail—there was no program, nothing to do her justice.
Alvin	I didn't want her to go to jail because I didn't believe she'd change. I sent her letters to plead, beg, pray she'd change. I guess some of them worked.
Alisha	I always believed she'd change.
Alvin	I was nine when she went to prison. I was ready because she sent us to Grandma's when she knew where the path was heading.
Alisha	We went to see her at Kankakee for Christmas. We didn't have a Christmas even though we had little kids. We had no tree, no presents. But it was good to see her.
Leona	I dropped out of high school. I got a scholarship to Truman College after I finished my GED with very high scores, but I couldn't take it because I got to work. I just missed to be the valedictorian of our class. I work for my daddy at the not-for-profit Lawndale Community newspaper. I do layout, administrative work. My daddy wanted an information source for people coming out of jail. He wrote a grant—he's so smart. He's been clean for 8 years.
	When Mama went to prison we was living with our cousin. The cousin put us out. She was addicted, too. I was crying because I didn't want to have to go to the shelter on Belmont and Clark. But I had to go with my sister. We were there four and a half months. I liked it better than Grandma's. Kids there had nowhere to go but the streets. I got kicked out of the shelter for fighting a girl who stole my pants—kids there had no clothes. This girl slept on a bench along Lake Michigan.
Alisha	Those days when Mama was doing drugs—I hated. I had no shoes, no bus fare to start high school. She promised me money for school but . . . I didn't start high school for three months. I went and stayed with my aunt.

When we stayed in Waukegan we went days without eating. When we did eat it was peanut butter and sugar bread. Mama got credit from the store until my brother stole. So then I always went to school because we got a good lunch.

Leona   I only went to school for first period. I made up a different doctor to get out of school—sometimes an eye doctor, sometimes a foot doctor. One day the teacher said she'd call my Mama, but I didn't care cause we had no phone.

Alvin   In summer when we needed bikes we stole them from the rich people. When the bikes caught a flat we had no money to fix the patches.

Alisha   We stole a lot . . . every day at the store. Once in Chicago Leona was selling drugs out of the house because my mama was doing drugs bad and we had to stay with my cousin who was awful. Leona had to drop out of school. We had no choice but to sell the drugs because we had nothing.

These children's survival strategies are held to standards they can't possibly uphold. Researcher Peggy McIntosh has shown that white privilege is as invisible to its beneficiaries as the relentless stripping of options is for those without class, race, and gender advantages. Joanetta and her children are neither lamenting the hand they've been dealt, nor blaming a culture that demonizes them. They are doing what they've always done—struggling to survive, alone, knowing there will not be support if they slip. For Joanetta's family, individual and collective survival is a victory when every social indicator would have predicted family and individual disintegration.

CONFRONTING VIOLENCE, DEATH, AND LOSS

The death of their brother Jackie deeply affected this family, none more so than its most vulnerable member, Ringer. He is the child of Joanetta's teenage pregnancy before she met Darnell, the father of the others. Ringer has always felt like an outsider, yet he is deeply connected to his family. Jackie's killing left Ringer bereft and fatalistic. As the oldest, he felt his task was to make sure his younger brother Jackie did not make the mistakes he made. When he couldn't protect the brother he loved, he gave up. He seems more defeated than hardened.

Leona   Our brother Jackie was very shy. He was a star on the basketball team at Acorn, then he went to Marshall High School. Everybody at school had nice clothes, so he needed them too. He started making money selling, so he quit high school. He wasn't using, except weed.

Ringer When we lived in Waukegan I had to turn myself in to the police because I shot a BB gun that hit a fire hydrant, bounced off, and hit a girl in the eye. I went to the juvenile home for eight months, then I went to a foster home.

When I came back from Waukegan and I saw that Jackie had all these good shoes, I told him not to drop out of school or he'd end up like me.

Alvin (The night) Jackie was killed he hung out with guys he didn't know. They were smoking blunts (marijuana) in a stolen car, but he didn't know it. The guy whose car had been stolen had been following the car driven by my brother's new friend. He was killed by mistake . . . but the guy who did it said he was fixin' to kill somebody. He was shot three times. His brains were shot out.

I had just got back from athletic camp that night to learn he was killed. I didn't cry because I thought he was just shot in the arm. When I saw him in the hospital I broke down.

I was doing good, but after [his death] my grades went bad. I had no attention span. I dropped basketball. My brother's friends said "Take his place. You look like him. We've got your back." But I wasn't that messed up to take the offer.

Ringer I'm just getting myself together. My mama don't understand how bad my brother's death has affected me. It should have been me killed. He had a chance to make it out. Maybe it was for a reason or maybe his death was supposed to change everybody's life.

Leona My sister stopped weed after Jackie's death. I stopped after I was pregnant. Maybe you, Ringer, have a weak will. You've been to prison for three years and say you'll change, but you don't.

Ringer I went to prison in November of 1999. I beat up my girlfriend's brother because he called me names. I was addicted. I have a temper . . . I did this at the probation officer's office! I caught eight years but did only two because of boot camp. It was bad, but I had to come home because when my brother was killed I almost went crazy. I beat up people.

It hurt me when my mother went to jail because I was messed up. I had emotional problems. I kept it inside; that's why my temper was so bad. I was alone. I needed her and she wasn't there for me . . . she'd never been there for me anyway.

> She sent me letters but it didn't help because she wasn't there. I was still stuck at the point where everything was snatched from me. My mother being with their father . . . I felt left out. Their father paid attention only to them.

Leona and Alisha   Wait a minute, we got whupped with extension cords.

Ringer   I got beat . . . if you all did something, I got whupped.

Alisha   My grandfather whupped us for allowing a teddy bear's stuffing to come out. He hit us with an extension cord. But we fought him back. I wouldn't let him hit my brother with that extension cord.

Ringer   He hated me because I almost killed their son [Ringer's stepfather]. He knocked my mother's arm out of place, so I got my friends and we knocked him out.

Joanetta   When I took parenting classes I realized I wasn't supposed to whup.

Leona   I won't whup my kids—no whupping.

MARKED FOR LIFE: STIGMA AND PLUCK

Whether these young people see themselves as branded like their mother, like Ringer, or whether they become compensatory, determined to avoid the pitfalls of prison and addiction, like Leona, they still bear the stigma of their past. The conditions that led to their mother's addiction continues to surround them. Leona insists that her children will never be "whupped," and she insists that nothing can ever persuade her to do drugs, but she is a single parent with three children who will grow up protecting each other as her brother Ringer protected her from the dangers of a west side abandoned by hope. How will she keep her boys from other "whuppins" or safe from schools where every student knows they will likely never make it out of the west side, where gangs vie for the only capital that flows toward the west side? Will her strength be enough? Will she be tempted to whup the boys into compliance for their safety? If her meager salary cannot feed her small family, if she cannot return to college to better herself, will this young woman, who was almost class valedictorian and who spent her childhood protecting her brothers and sisters, despair and turn to drugs?

Leona met despair as a young child and she chose survival and a steadiness that everyone depended on. She insists she won't veer from that path, yet the context of her refusing "whuppins," of telling the truth even when it's painful, is a context so stacked against her best efforts that her triumph will be a small miracle.

That one mother, Joanetta, was addicted and that another mother, her daughter Leona, refused addiction, is the "text" that dominant culture reads while averting its gaze from the social inequities that undercut both mothers at every turn. Policy makers have stigmatized mothers like Joanetta as radically different from "normal" women. The abdication of their mothering role is considered all but incomprehensible, but the state's "protective" response to her children amounts to "neglect and abuse," which is more damaging. This state failure, however, remains hidden because it is embedded in policy decisions that relegate the children of the poor to life opportunities that guarantee social exclusion. Like their mother, the children are considered expendable.

RINGER'S DESPAIR

Alvin, Alisha, and Leona have fought against their expendability, but Ringer believes the stigmas that have been forced on him. In spite of the fact that he, like his siblings, scored high on school exams, and that before he dropped out of high school he was an excellent athlete who took third in the state in cross country, Ringer has little confidence in himself. Although no one said it, it was clear they were terrified that something tragic could happen to Ringer. Though he denied being a gang member, Joanetta insists that he is still affiliated. He attributes his initial gang involvement with his need to protect his sister.

> I was thirteen when I got initiated into a gang. When my sister (Leona) lost her hair I had to leave school early to pick her up so nobody messed with her. I had to fight every day for her . . . kids who'd pull her scarf off. It messed me up that I had to leave school one hour early every day. One time I got into a fight with a gang-banger—a guy who killed people—I had to fight him because of what he did to my sister. After that nobody messed with me.

Ringer was living with Joanetta at the time of the interview. He wasn't working because he could do better selling on the streets. Given the job opportunities for young black males, his assessment, though dangerous and heartbreaking to his family, was not a depraved, thuggish choice. He kept telling his mother he was not selling, which she didn't believe.

Joanetta, who was calm with everyone, flared at him, confronting his continued use of drugs. Then Alisha defended him, breaking down, almost begging her mother not to hurt him. Joanetta grew tougher, as if any response that gave an inch to Ringer was enablement.

Ringer   (responding to Joanetta's confronting him about his habit) You don't even remember me playing sports. You don't know I have my GED. You worship the ground they walk on.

Alisha   It hurts me when Mama says bad things to Ringer.

Leona   They's always one child who follows they Mama. Maybe he won't do right without being told (the truth).

Alisha is crying now, but Joanetta is dry-eyed and tough.

Joanetta   You are used to hustling, Ringer. You learned it from me. You don't show nothin' different. You have an addiction you have no control over. Yeah, maybe God did send you this lady (pointing to herself) for a reason. Ain't nobody got us this far except God. You have to want to live for yourself. What I wrote to you in prison is about what I learned and I got it the hard way. Ain't no one going nowhere with drugs. I know what I did to you. You have to give, Ringer, to get. I chose—chose to be here for you. Do stuff from your heart, not to receive.

Ringer   (turns to address me) My stepfather made her choose him over me.

Alisha   (crying hard) You have to give him a chance, Mama.

Leona   He's had a chance. He doesn't take care of the children he's had with Lola.

Ringer   Lola cut me with a knife. Yeah, I pulled a gun on her because I got the kids candy and she was mad. She was mad too because I wouldn't have sex with her. She was little and pregnant and I was afraid for her.

Joanetta   I think he was high.

Ringer   (addressing me) My daddy was an alcoholic.

Alisha   (seems to be pleading) Mama . . .

Ringer pulls his chair back but remains silent. After a few minutes of silence, he puts forward his last plea.

Ringer   Maybe it was meant for Mama to get herself together . . . I mean, she is our mama. But she's got to give me a chance. Everybody has a choice. Look how long it took her to get it together. Look at all I've been through. Jackie . . . you don't know how it affected me. You see me every day, but you don't know what I'm feeling.

GENDER IMPRISONMENT

Joanetta seems to be the one family member who obliquely sees that her role as a wife and mother shaped her addiction. Her children say little about their father's imprisonment, his other family, or the addiction that prevented him from supporting them. Internalizing the culture's gender standards, Joanetta's family holds her responsible for both their survival and their unraveling. Joanetta's children are unsparing in revealing the pain her addiction cost them. Underlying their stories is a degradation they don't identify—poverty that stalked their mother's own childhood and theirs. In spite of her addiction, their mother kept a roof over their heads until she lost custody of her children to her mother-in-law. Only their mother identifies another degradation—her husband's control. "I never asked what I wanted from life . . . Darnell told me how life should be."

Researcher Beth Ritchie believes that legally incarcerated women are victims of gender incarceration before they ever reach a prison or jail cell. As a result of her work with women at Rikers Island Prison, Ritchie identified the physical or sexual violence experienced by women, in particular African-American women, as a gender trap that compels them to crime. These women, ignored by mainstream culture and policy analysts, have also too often been invisible to feminist antiviolence workers and researchers. According to Ritchie, African-American women "exist in a social world that was determined to condemn them, only to be exiled from the broader society that failed to deliver promised opportunity and rewards. To this, add the social context of an unresponsive social service system, a mean spirited and repressive public welfare agenda, increasingly aggressive law enforcement policies, and growing social intolerance for women who cannot fit in to dominant society . . . and their gender entrapment becomes clearer."[2]

Entrapment is about a lack of choices. White middle-class ideology assumes a variety of choices that permit a self-determining subjectivity. The entrapment net that catches poor mothers also sweeps up their children. Gender is a trap for poor battered women, but the impoverished west side of Chicago, for all of its people's courage, is a trap, too. What choice does Ringer have? What choice does Joanetta have in "saving" him? It is true that Ringer has no chance until he kicks drugs?

But what are his chances even then? He is battered by a system that has written him off; he is an ex-con with little hope of finding decent paying work; his "weakness" is that he believes the stereotypes that have been forced on him.

Social policy makers invariably "read" Ringer's text, as well as Joanetta's, from a "deficit assessment" model of interpretation. Historically, America's policy makers stigmatize the poor, but if the texts are read from sociologist John McKnight's asset model, another story emerges. It is the story of a family's courage and resourcefulness when confronted with all but impossible odds. An asset model simply shifts interpretation and policy from investigation of a family's deficits to identifying the family's assets. Current policy sees the stigmatized as families who need "services" in order to conform to middle-class, white standards of family life. McKnight's asset model begins with the family's strengths, in spite of evident problems. Because the focus is not on family pathology, structural failure can be addressed. Moreover, for families overwhelmed by social exclusion, asset-based policies would offer support identified as necessary by those families who need support, not by bureaucracies created to spot failure, such as the child welfare system. Asset-based policies not only disrupt the current dependency model by creating partnerships focused on strengths instead of weaknesses, they also foster social sufficiency and hope.

Except for Ringer, Joanetta's children have hopes. They have managed to stay together and to place enormous faith in their youngest sibling, Alvin, to "make it" to college. Realists, they have redirected childhood dreams within the limited options they have. It is poignant to hear Alisha reflect on the dreams they had as children: "When she was on drugs, Mama would put us in a room and we'd talk about things. My brothers and Leona used to talk after we got whupped and we said we'll never grow up and do drugs. The boys would say they wanted to be doctors. I wanted to be a lawyer. Alvin wanted to be a football player."

Listening to them, Joanetta said with sorrow and honesty: "They all had to figure out how to survive. When they saw my addiction was not going to change, they would talk and figure out how to support and to feed each other."

The dilemma for Joanetta and her children is clear: How do we survive in a world where the choices offered are not transformative? Confronted by poverty, addiction, and inadequate education, their victory is the fact that they survived as a family and continue to cling to each other in spite of the wounds they carry.

4

FAMILY NARRATIVES OF SURVIVAL AND SORROW: BELL, MELVANIE, NADIA, AND LOUELLA

You can destroy a whole family by taking a mother away. It's like giving a family a death sentence. We can't enslave Blacks anymore but we can destroy their families. When have we ever supported Black family life?

Sister Kathy Nolan, O.P. [1]

How should we judge an American practice that produces a new generation of devastated and shattered children every year? What judgment is reserved for this national practice that turns on children as they enter an adulthood that will be haunted, and too often is a repetition of the very lives governing authorities impotently and hypocritically cajole against? This is the current United States policy of incarcerating mothers for nonviolent crimes and ignoring the traumatic impact on their children. We could label the practice a moral crime. Most prisons do not even request information about a woman's children when she is sent through classification. The children are mostly invisible to the penal system. They gain social significance only if they are arrested in later life.

Addicted mothers, already filled with guilt for their failures, must battle the demon of their addiction. If arrested, they have to make Solomon-like decisions about the fate of their children immediately,

29

and in the midst of crisis. Sometimes the mother herself, feeling guilty and confused and fearing that she cannot be trusted, will give up the child. This was the case for Bell.

When Bell was told her baby, Martin, tested positive for cocaine, she gave the baby to his paternal grandmother—not for foster care but for adoption. Now that she is in a transitional program after prison, she has gone to visit her son but he doesn't recognize her.

Martin knows I'm his mama but face-to-face he'll hide from me. He doesn't really know who I am and I don't know who he is. I think he's afraid of me at four years old. I just wasn't there for him. When I got clean I asked God for forgiveness. I never wanted to go to his home—I was afraid my heart would be broken.

Her daughter, Celine, has been suspended from school for fighting and telling teachers she'll "kick their ass."

She has an anger problem that she didn't have until she came to visit me in prison. When she had to leave she started to cry. After that she was mad all the time. Now that I can get her to open up to me—she's getting better. She's seven years old.

Bell's other son is with her mother in Alabama. Bell's mother has been clean of drugs for years. Bell herself endured her own mother's "going away" through drugs, and it seems Bell's daughter Celine's behavior was a response to being separated from her mother, too. But unlike Celine (Bell's seven-year-old daughter who acts out), Bell was the good daughter who took on responsibility for her family.

I couldn't stop mother's habit, but she kept a roof over our heads. When she gave birth to my baby brother, who was born with cocaine in his system, DCFS told her if she didn't get treatment, they would take us away. She went to treatment and I went with her as her support. My mama and I are close.

During my teen years I was taking care of the house, taking my brother to school, paying the bills, cleaning, and cooking. My mother was working at the airport and she'd leave on Thursday and not come home until Sunday. So I didn't have a childhood. I dropped out of school at seventeen.

The detail of her mother's work at the airport contextualizes the economic struggle of her single-parent mother. It can take up to two and a half hours to take public transportation to get to O'Hare Airport from Chicago's west side, which amounts to four hours travel time per day. Bell's mother, who was a cleaning lady at the airport, probably slept on chairs for the four days she worked each week. That's no longer possible because of a recent city ordinance that forbids anyone who is not on a delayed flight (read homeless people) from sleeping on the airport chairs.

Bell's own drug habit began when her boyfriend talked her into trying heroin. By then, ironically, her mother had gone into a treatment program and was a recovering addict. Her mother was deeply disappointed when she realized her daughter was following in her path. At that point they switched roles, with Bell's mother resuming child-rearing and domestic responsibility for the family.

Bell became pregnant at age eighteen and at nineteen and miscarried both times. She quit drugs for a year but met another man who introduced her to smoking crack. Her mother tried to stop her but according to Bell, the experience of seeing Bell wasted on drugs, "running the streets" caused her mother "to relapse trying to save me."

Her mother recovered again, but Bell did not. Pregnant again, Bell had her daughter at Bethany Hospital and they all lived with Bell's grandmother because her mother was unable to keep her job as a teacher's assistant at a child care agency and she couldn't afford rent for the family. Bell's habit continued through the birth of two more sons. Without skills Bell supported them the only way she knew—she sold drugs and continued using.

By 1997 Bell had given up. She gave birth to Martin in a crack house. "My baby was born breech. I thought I'd die. I panicked. But my mom had come to help me. She said to calm down, it was okay, and she delivered Martin. By the time the police came, he was lying on my chest."

Through tragedy upon tragedy, Bell and her mother were there for each other. The men in their lives were abusive or drug dealers. But after the birth of Martin in a crack house, Bell's mother saw that her daughter was out of control, and proceeded to make the best intervention she could. She moved to Alabama with Bell's first son. It was agreed that the baby, Martin, would go to the child's paternal grandmother, and Bell's daughter Celine would go with her great-grandmother. Bell went on the run for two years.

When Bell was arrested for a drug offense, they offered her boot camp—an intensive, punitive military-style training camp that cuts prison time served by sometimes 50 percent—but Bell refused the offer. She knew it would get her an early release but would not offer her a program that was intensive and long enough to kick her habit. She was incarcerated at Logan and then Decatur, where she went into a treatment program and received her GED and a sanitation license.

I see all the pain I caused my children and I won't go back to that life. I won't even take aspirin. I want to see my kids grow up. I won't force my children to live with me if they don't want to. I just want a relationship. I don't expect to jump into their lives and change all that they know. I have to be patient and trust them and myself.

My mom and I support each other in staying sober. We go to meetings together. My mother is so proud of me. I don't know what I'd do without her.

One can only imagine the road ahead for Bell and her children. Miraculously, although she and her mother devastated each other, they also saved each other. But what of Celine—already angry at seven years of age? How does a mother cope with trying to find a way back to children who are strangers? What tensions does it put on the caretakers and the mother to negotiate these wrenching relationships? What developmental impacts do these disruptions have on the lives of the children?

EFFECTS OF MOTHER'S INCARCERATION ON CHILDREN

Few studies explore the long-term effects of a mother's incarceration on children. None, for example, reveal how many will turn to drugs or alcohol in adulthood, how many will become homeless, how many will be suicidal, or how many will struggle with incapacitating depression or anxiety as a result of childhood trauma. Additionally, there are scant studies that measure the resilience of these children as adults.

About four in ten incarcerated women report prior physical or sexual abuse, not all of which occurred in childhood.[2] One in three women in prison has attempted suicide at some point in her life, and approximately one in five spent time as a ward of the state in a foster home or residential center.[3] Almost 20 percent of women were homeless the year before their incarceration, and 23 percent of the mothers reported mental illness.[4]

According to Franciscan Sister Patricia Schlosser, a social worker who works with women in transition from Illinois prisons, the reason so many women choose drugs or become suicidal is because they were sexually abused early in life.

One prisoner I knew was sexually abused by her father, then sexually abused by her priest. Later she was sexually abused because she was an addict and to pay for her habit she prostituted herself. She said she used drugs in order to go numb, so she couldn't think. She's been in and out of prison three or four times.

A lot of the women get into drugs because of a man. That's the sad part. The women get high because they can't make it in this society. Even those who sell drugs just want clothes, a car, a house. It's a desire to get out of poverty. They say to me, "I gave my kids everything they wanted, except I didn't give them myself."[5]

There are studies that tell us about the childhoods of women prisoners, though we should not take their mother's experiences to be predictive of theirs. First of all, it is not possible to measure the force and unpredictability of the human will and spirit. In addition, a number of factors—such as supportive families and communities, participation in transition or rehabilitation programs that are sufficiently long, and opportunities to find decent paying jobs—can break the cycle of trauma and victimization. Yet a context that includes social inequality, racial exclusion, poverty, and community disintegration continues to press upon each generation of the poor.

The majority of incarcerated mothers came from single-parent homes in which at least one family member had been incarcerated. Not surprisingly, two studies by researcher Denise Johnston, M.D., indicate that the children of incarcerated parents are more likely candidates for future incarceration than other children. The "Children of Offenders Study (1992, 1993) indicates that 29 percent of the 11 to 14 year olds had been arrested or incarcerated, [and] the Jailed Mothers Study (1991) found that 11.4 percent of children of participating women had been arrested and 10 percent had been incarcerated."[6]

According to Sister Patricia Schlosser, imprisoned mothers are consumed with guilt about their children, especially if the children end up in prison.

Mothers blame themselves because their kids go to prison. But part of the reason is not just the influence of being around parents who are addicted, it's also that their incarceration separates them when their kids needed them most.

One woman I knew had been married to an abusive police officer whom she reported many times. One day she ran into an alley because he was chasing her with a gun. He was killed. I don't know if she grabbed his gun or what. She felt horrible but thought she'd be understood because of the previous pattern of complaints. But no, she got ten years. She couldn't believe it. Though religious, she felt abandoned by God. She said she missed every important event in her children's lives—every prom, graduation, confirmation, and wedding. When she was released they were all grown and they still cry about this. She can never reclaim the losses of her family's threshold events.[7]

CREATING A NEW ARMY OF THE DISENFRANCHISED: TERMINATION OF PARENTAL RIGHTS

Not all incarcerated mothers are fortunate enough to have a relative who will care for their children. In fact, it is often the most vulnerable and isolated single parents whose children are taken into state custody to be cared for by strangers. A mother who has no relative she can turn to at the time of her arrest will typically have officers take her children to a child welfare office or residential center for placement.

Children are often punished more severely than their convicted mother. I once saw two brothers, six and seven years old, waiting outside a caseworker's office at a DCFS intake center. They sat with their small duffle bags of clothes, kicking their legs back and forth, their faces bewildered and frightened. They did not know at that moment that their lives had become unalterably changed. Not only had they lost their mother for a critical period in their childhood, but within a few hours or days they would lose each other as well. Siblings are rarely placed together in foster care. Most tragically of all, the permanent loss of a child's family of origin occurs when parental rights are terminated. For those two little brothers, the wait for processing outside the caseworker's office marked the beginning of their own institutionalization.

The reason that termination of parental rights occurs is that incarcerated mothers are often presumed unfit by virtue of their conviction, and the process of reunification hangs on the mother's ability to prove her fitness. Philip Genty points out: "The constitutional requirement that parental 'unfitness' be proven before rights can be permanently terminated does not answer the question of what amounts to 'unfitness.'"[8] A key factor indicating fitness is a mother's ongoing visits with her child. "Continuing contact between parent and child is perhaps the most significant predictor of family reunification, following parental incarceration."[9]

When the prison is a couple of hours away, the odds that a child's foster parent will be willing or able to spend an entire day taking the child to visit his or her mother in prison are not high. If the child is well behaved, the foster parents may wish the mother's parental rights to be terminated so they can perhaps adopt the child. The foster family may feel anger at the mother for "abandoning" her child, and may therefore not wish the child to be involved with an unfit mother. If the children respond to the trauma and grief of loss by acting out or withdrawing, as is more typically the case, the foster parents may feel disconnected from them and less responsive to their needs, particularly their need for their mother.

The children's original trauma may predate their parent's incarceration. They have already faced disruptions and crises related to their mother's abuse or due to her drug addiction. In spite of these traumatic episodes, most abused or addicted mothers love their children. The trauma of losing their mother catapults children into a grief or rage that few child care experts, juvenile court judges, or criminal justice agents have identified or treated. The children's pain becomes invisible, as do the children themselves.

Dominican Sister Kathy Nolan has been a social worker at Grace House, a Chicago transition program for former women inmates, for seven years. She says she has attended too many court hearings requested by DCFS in which a mother had her parental rights terminated. A common reason given for termination is the fact that the particular mother had little contact with her child while she was in prison, despite the fact that the frequency of visits depends on factors beyond her control. According to Kathy Nolan,

> If a woman goes to prison, DCFS rarely tries to contact her. DCFS punishes the woman for not living up to her maternal role. Occasionally a caseworker is compassionate, but that is rare. Typically they don't answer phone calls, change meeting dates, and fail to inform mothers about upcoming hearings. If the mother does not show up for the hearing, she loses her kids. There is a lot of pressure for women to terminate their parental responsibilities— often they feel beaten up by the system, and they just give up.[10]

According to attorney Gail Smith, director of Chicago Legal Advocacy for Incarcerated Mothers (CLAIM), the lack of coordination between child welfare agencies and departments of corrections "create(s) nearly insurmountable obstacles to parents who wish to preserve their parental rights and reunite with their families."[11] As an example of the obstacles, Smith relates that mothers typically seem to be systematically excluded from critical decisions about children's futures. She says, "It is common for foster care agencies to exclude mothers from the planning process and the semi-annual agency assessments [often called administrative case reviews] that establish the service plan [for the child] for the next six months."[12]

Few mothers have legal advocates in these termination proceedings. Kathy Nolan has accompanied many mothers to court, and she claims that she couldn't get through the ordeal without an advocate if she were in the mother's shoes. Going to juvenile court can be extremely intimidating for mothers who feel helpless and ignored, and who do not know their rights.

Often mothers are either not informed of termination hearings or they are not informed in a way that helps them pursue the paperwork and logistical support that would allow them to appear at the hearings. This is not simply a Cook County, Illinois problem. Twenty-five states have statues for termination of parental rights that are directed at incarcerated parents.[13]

In addition, the termination policy is very short-sighted. The kids always carry abandonment issues and feel the situation is their fault. When they hit their teenage years they are filled with rage and rejection. According to Kathy Nolan, "The system creates a new army of disenfranchised and disempowered people."[14]

A mother may have her children placed in foster care, which increases the possibility of termination of parental rights, because child welfare agencies will not place children with relatives who have criminal records. According to Katherine Gabel and Denise Johnston, "Given the reality that approximately half of all incarcerated females have an immediate family member who has been incarcerated, and that the goal of agency services is to reunite the child with a parent who is an offender, such guidelines are unduly restrictive and increase the number of children of women prisoners who enter foster care with strangers."[15]

RELATIVE FOSTER CARE: BROKEN HEARTS, BRAVE HEARTS

Children placed with a relative, usually a grandmother, are luckier than the children placed with strangers, but nothing prepares a grandmother for the effects of trauma carried by the children when they enter her apartment to spend an average of four years—almost one-third of their childhood. Neither the child welfare system nor the criminal justice system provides the newly formed family with support. They are on their own to deal with trauma.

In Illinois, the DCFS will intervene if the grandmother says she can't continue to deal with one or more of the children. They will send the child to other relatives, or if none exist, they'll be sent to nonrelative foster parents. In most states, neither child welfare nor the criminal justice system will offer the family transportation to the prison. They do not offer joint counseling for parents and children related to their loss and separation. They do not provide the parent's attorney with advice about her own or her children's legal rights. They do not pay for tutorial help when the full weight of the loss settles in and children's moods and grades nose-dive. They do not pay for after-school care if Grandma has to work. If the grandmother requests it, they will have a counselor speak with the family, but the family must be able to travel to a central office for those services.

Unless there is a catastrophe or repeated requests from Grandma, an overworked caseworker will make perfunctory checks and assume the family is doing okay on the small financial payments made to relative caretakers. Most grandmothers do not ask for help out of fear that the kids will be taken away if it appears they are not managing well. When individual caseworkers from child welfare or social workers within the prison do try to be family advocates and take on the weight of their own bureaucratic culture they may, sadly, confront lack of cooperation from the family. The sum of previous experiences has taught the family to fear or disdain caseworkers.

MELVANIE AND HER DAUGHTERS

Melvanie, a former addict who used drugs for years and who spent years in Illinois prisons, is a direct, no-nonsense mother of three daughters. Currently she is a case manager with Jump Start at the University of Illinois in Chicago. When I spoke with her, she suggested I speak with her girls separately so that they might feel free to speak their minds about the eight years of separation from her, including some preprison years when the state took custody, and some years in prison. Even though the interviews were separate, in the section that follows I have interspersed Melvanie's reflections with her daughters whenever her comments and theirs converged on a particular subject.

Melvanie's life changed when her mother unwittingly turned her in to the Cook County DCFS. Melvanie's mother told the caseworker that her daughter was using drugs. As a result, Melvanie's three daughters, Tanisha (twelve years old), Janisha (seven), and Raynisha (two), were placed with their grandmother. Tanisha never forgave her grandmother.

Tanisha   When Grandma called DCFS everything changed. My mother never abused us. We knew she was using. But after DCFS came my mother wasn't around because of the rules of the state. She couldn't see us until they gave her permission. After that she was more out in the streets and she really went bad as far as drugs.

Melvanie When they put my kids in the system I went to treatment for thirty days. I thought the kids would come home. I didn't know it was a long process. For two weeks I didn't use but when I realized I wouldn't get my kids back, I gave up.

After I lost my kids I was so angry and hurt. I would wake up crying that I didn't have my kids. Then I really started using. I went down. Nothing mattered to me anymore. I loved my kids.

Tanisha I was really disgusted with my grandmother because my mother wasn't neglectful. I thought she called DCFS just for the money.

Melvanie I was angry with my mother. But actually my mother didn't call DCFS to turn me in. She thought DCFS would come over and talk to me. My mother is from down South and she only went to fourth grade. She was uneducated and didn't know better.

[What happened was] that I left my kid's father and went to my mother's house. My partner was abusive sexually, physically, and verbally. He had a temper. After a week or more at my mother's I went to see him. That's when I started slacking up on being with the kids. My mother got angry and threatened to call DCFS. When she did, she told me to go over to meet with the guy at DCFS. He asked me if I used and I said yes. Then they put me under the title of abandonment, which was not true. Then they took temporary custody.

My mother apologized and said if she knew what would happen she'd never have called. But it took me years to forgive her. I was the type who never talked back to my mother. I was a good child.

Tanisha When I couldn't get along with my grandma DCFS changed me to my other grandma.

Janisha I was changed by DCFS four times. I didn't get along with my grandma and I wanted to be with my sister. I was changed to my aunt for one year, but she was mean. Then they changed me to another aunt, but I didn't like her either. My aunts took care of us, but there was no connection. What I really wanted was my mother.

Tanisha It was easy to get into DCFS but *hard* to get out. A lot of going to court. Every three months. Case workers kept giving us a continuance. My mother had to do certain things—get in a program, get a job, etc. This isn't a quick process. Getting your kids back takes years.

Melvanie admitted herself into Grace House in order to overcome her habit and center herself. She was so efficient, straightforward, and supportive of others that Grace House asked her to be on the staff. She was house manager for four years. Melvanie was determined to get her girls back after she returned from prison, in spite of the fact that they'd spent as much of their childhood with relatives as with her. Still, they longed for the time when they could be with their mother, even though by the time she returned, two of her daughters were themselves single parents.

Tanisha and Raynisha both lived with their paternal grandmother, and their youngest sister stayed with her maternal grandmother, the "mother" who raised her, because she was a toddler when DCFS intervened. Currently Melvanie's two youngest daughters, her grandchild, and her daughter's partner live with her. In the section that follows, all three of the daughters describe the effects that the loss of their mother had on their lives, and their relationship with DCFS.

Tanisha   The first two caseworkers seemed to show interest in our family because they were doing more than just a job. To me, though, with DCFS, there's too much you have to go through. We went through so much. They aren't helping those who need them. I hate them . . . I won't say, them, I'll say I hate their guidelines and rules. It's ridiculous. It took my mother two years to get Raynisha back. I was eleven.

Janisha   When my mom got out I was seventeen. At first I stayed with my grandma. I didn't hold anything against my mom, I just didn't want to be moved again.

Tanisha   [When mother got out] I was already living on my own. I was in independent living where DCFS pays for an apartment until you are twenty-one—it's a place for teen moms.

Right now today, it still hurts me that I have to say "Grandma" not my "mom." That's a hurting feeling. My mom and I are very close. I don't think I'd have two kids [if my mom were left with us]. I was just looking for love. I mean I love my kids but I just don't know.

Janisha   Here's how it [mother's incarceration] affected me. I dropped out of high school. I went to three different high schools. I kept ditching school and kept getting kicked out. Then I went to an alternative school, but because I messed up before, I didn't have enough credits to graduate. But I continued and then three classes before I was to graduate I ended up getting pregnant and couldn't finish. My little girl is three.

I blame myself for not finishing. I'm not so smart, but I'm not dumb either.

By our being separated I'm not as close to my little sister. She thinks I'm mean. I believe when we were together we were close, but once we got separated, it created a distance.

Tanisha As for our little sister Raynisha, after my mother left, at night she wet the bed for two years.

Janisha It's all just made me stronger. I'll never go through drugs. I've seen enough. I'll never let my kids go through what we went through.

Tanisha I work at Sears. My kids have two fathers, but I'm a single parent.

Janisha I don't work, but I'm with my child's father.

Raynisha [I live with my mom] and I'm a sophomore in high school.

Janisha She's doing better in school this year.

Melvanie I'm appreciative that my sisters took my girls in, but they didn't give them enough schooling support. My not being there to help them with homework affected their schoolwork. That's why we put my youngest, Raynisha, in private school for her last two years of grade school. My youngest lacks self-esteem and she keeps trying to fit in.

My middle daughter is a good mother but she lacks motivation. She needs to finish school and get a job. She needs "push." You have to set an example. She's tired of my talking to her. I've given her to God's care.

My oldest has a high school diploma and I'm so proud of her. I often wondered, "What is going on inside her?"

VISITATION: A HURTIN' FEELING

Melvanie's oldest, Tanisha, describes the years of her mother's addiction as a time when her mother was "more like a sister," and Tanisha struggled to keep all of them together. She was devoted to her mother, and it seems she kept her own pain inside so as not to be a burden. In particular, she kept complaints to herself when she visited her mother in prison. Visitation was painful for all of them but was also the glue that kept them together. Melvanie describes her ambivalence and longing when they came to visit.

Melvanie To be honest, the first time they came to visit I didn't know what to feel. The closer the day of their arrival, I wasn't sure I wanted them to come and see me in a prison but my desire for them and their need for me overcame my anxiety. . . . Actually, the hardest thing was when they'd phone me and I couldn't see them.

Tanisha I visited my mom at Dwight prison and it gave me a hurtin' feeling to see her. To me, it was sad. But she had to be in a [drug] program. I was glad she was in programs.

Janisha I was sad to see her but happy because if she didn't go there she wouldn't have gotten us back.

Actually, if her children didn't visit her in prison, Melvanie might not have gotten them back at all. What typically saves families like Melvanie's is their love for each other. Even when love is filled with mistakes and hurts, it is still what keeps families together. The story of this family's reunification had much to do with the bonds that caused Melvanie's children to come see her even when they were intimidated by going to the prison. Those same bonds encouraged her mother and sisters to take the long trip to Dwight Prison so that she and her children could spend an hour or two together.

BREAKING BONDS: NO VISITS

According to a Bureau of Justice report, more than half of mothers in state prisons never receive a visit from their children.[16] When a mother has the opportunity to say good-bye to her children before being sent to prison, she invariably reassures them that they will see each other soon. Unwittingly she offers false hope. The majority of children who visit do so rarely and sporadically. As I have discussed, there are several reasons for this.

Sixty percent of inmates report that their prison is 100 miles away from where their children live.[17] Relative caretakers lack transportation or travel funds for visits to the prison. Foster parents do not have a stake in making lengthy trips, and often caretakers don't have anyone to care for the other children in their care. Moreover, if children and caretakers do make one visit, the experience can be so unsettling that they won't repeat it. Sister Patricia Schlosser describes Mother's Day at the women's prison in Kankakee, Illinois: "They searched everyone for so long, causing such a delay that many children and their care-takers couldn't get in before visiting hours were up. The prison system is all law, it does nothing to help families. Some individuals do but the system doesn't support them."[18]

Caretakers often won't return for visits after their first experience because they may fear the process traumatizes the children even more. Children must be frisked, sent through metal detectors, and made to wait and wait. Often, older children return from the visit angry, hurt, and embittered. Upon leaving, younger children cry, have repeated bed-wetting episodes, and perform poorly at school. In spite of these risks, advocates insist that contact visits with a mother maintains bonds and is a key determinant in whether or not parental rights of the mother are terminated or maintained.

Based on her work with such families, Sister Patricia understands why so few grandmothers bring the children to Kankakee (Kankakee is only an hour from Chicago; Dwight, the largest Illinois women's prison, is a full two hours away).

Grandma, who usually has the kids, often resents her daughter. She is raising a second family of kids who are angry and some have dropped out of school. She's had to quit her job to watch them and has lost income. So here's Grandma, late in her life, giving up the little savings she's had paying for shoes and jackets. She can barely keep up and she's angry. Sometimes she says too much to the kids about their mom.

The grandmother may not have a phone, or may put a block on her phone because she can't afford the long distance phone bills from Mom. Women make only $15 a month in prison and can't afford to make desperately needed phone calls to their children. It's tough on everybody . . . nothing in prisons helps maintain family bonds.[19]

THE GENEROSITY OF CARETAKERS

Most caretakers of children of incarcerated mothers, whether relatives or foster parents, though often overburdened and resentful, have taken children in because they are committed and caring people. Nadia responded when her sister-in-law Louella was incarcerated, but she will never receive a citizen's award for her generosity. She lives in the heart of Lawndale, where gritty apartment buildings stand alone, surrounded by open lots of rusted drums and auto wreckage. Along Roosevelt Road, grimy steel-barred storefront windows wink sadly into the sun.

In 1994 Nadia took in Louella's children, Janine (twelve years old), Bobo (ten), and Ralph (nine) when their grandmother, who'd tried unsuccessfully to care for them for two years, was going to let DCFS take them.

I told her "No, don't put them there they'll get lost." Suddenly I had five children. It was tough getting money for kids who are not yours. DCFS said, "If you abuse them we can give you help, otherwise we can't." I got food stamps for the two boys, but I had to go to court to get guardianship for Janine, the oldest. But once I started work they cut me off food stamps—nothing.

When the kids came to me they had not seen their mother for almost two years. I got them into school and took them to see their mother. They'd get very nervous and then they'd cry to see her. They cried in the bus coming home. They only saw their mother for two hours every other month. I took all five kids with me to see her. I tried to keep this family together. I tried to keep them in touch with her through the phone. That was the only part of her that they had. They were good kids, but they were angry and hurt. I didn't allow them to run the streets. We played games in the house. In the winter I kept them indoors. Sometimes we went to the Smorgasbord. In the summer we went to Douglas Park or the beach.

They missed their mother so much. Bobo started getting suspended from class and I'd have to miss work to go to school to see what's going on. Janine acted out too, but she's a straight-A student. She wanted to be the boy's mother. She was going to drop out of school to take care of the boys. I told her, "That's not your responsibility, I'll take care of these children."

Their father, my brother, never came to see these kids . . . twice, three times. He's still getting high. Their mother loved her kids. She needed help, not jail. She would have done the same thing for me.

Nadia's strength and generosity has been a source of healing for Janine. Janine's mother, Louella, a shy and timid person, has none of Nadia's sense of confidence and authority. Janine resents Louella for leaving and for not being Nadia. She's afraid her mother won't have the strength to handle her family. She's afraid her own childhood will be over and that she won't be able to go to college—her one dream. Nadia invited Louella to live with her for a time until she could get a job, find an apartment and reassure her children that they could be a family together and make it on their own. Nadia knows how cruel her brother was to Louella, and knows how both her brother and prison have broken her. She tried to help this family find its way forward.

Nadia was afraid that Louella might be too depressed to care for the children when she finally moved into her own apartment. Nadia didn't know how to get her the help she needed. Within months of looking for work, Louella returned to her abusive husband and then she returned to drinking.

I'm just so disappointed in her. Her oldest daughter won't leave me, and her boys, who are sweet boys, are just left to hit the streets. They all are over here every weekend, but the boys are reaching teen years and they know I have rules and at their mother's there are no rules. I'm afraid for the oldest if he ever gets in trouble because he's a gentle boy and jail would destroy him.

Prison seems to have changed Louella, a timid person, for the worse. I just feel like Louella never received help for her depression or her problems and she fell back to the only life she knew. For instance, returning to my brother—he's no good. But Louella always seems crazy about the people who hurt her most, and she's mean to her kids who love her. She loves her mother who treated her terrible. Maybe it's all she knows, I don't know. Or maybe something affected her brain when she was nine years old. Her mother had a boyfriend who used to beat her, and when the police came Louella's mother said, "Don't open the door." But she was so little and when the police yelled, she opened the door. When the police left, Louella's mother took out a hammer and hit her in the head with it.

Even for the strongest mothers, returning to a world of poverty and isolation, compounded by the problems of reclaiming their children's trust, reintegration is a herculean task. Not every mother can be as clear about the past and the future as Melvanie.

I worry about my Raynisha and I worry about what I've caused all my children. But I don't know how to tell them it's not just that I can't change the past, it's that without the past I wouldn't be who I've become. So I know they have to make their own way and value their own mistakes or they can't become.

5

EXPENDABLE BODIES, RACIALIZED POLICIES

Because some bodies fail to conform physiologically, different bodies are expected and therefore required to behave differently under state or police gaze. Greater obedience is demanded of those whose physical difference marks them aberrational, offensive or threatening.

Joy James[1]

There comes those moments of despair . . . America has no desire for your presence or any need for your people. How else, you ask yourself, can one explain the death and debilitation from drugs and disease, the incarceration of whole generations of your men, the consignment of millions of women and children to half-lives of poverty and dependence.

Andrew Hacker[2]

With the passage of President Reagan's Anti-Drug Abuse Act in 1986, a war on drugs became a war on poor women of color. The war never captured the big-fish dealers; instead, it was aimed at low-level street users and sellers—the small fish: poor blacks, Latinos, the young, and women. In 1997, seventy-five percent of those convicted for drug crimes in state prisons had no previous convictions for violent crimes.[3] If law and policy makers were interested in a reduction in drug use, they aimed at the wrong targets. But if surveillance and punishment

45

were spectacles intended to enforce gender and race standards, they had deadly aim. Between 1986 and 1991, African-American women's incarceration in state prisons for drug offenses increased 828 percent, Latino women's increased 328 percent and white women's increased 241 percent.[4] The majority of these women were single mothers punished for their failure to represent maternal integrity and family values.

Historically in America the unfit mother has played the leading role in a theater of blame. No unfit mother has evoked more social condemnation than the pregnant black crackhead. In the theatrics of punishment, the reason given for incarcerating women crack users, particularly mothers, is the need to protect fetuses or vulnerable children. Yet the most damaging threats to these children are ignored daily. For example, in the 1980s and early 1990s, public outrage erupted against callous, pregnant crack addicts who bore low-birth-weight crack babies. While it is true that cocaine ingestion during pregnancy does cause low birth weight in newborns, a 1985 medical report listed 40 other issues that can cause low birth weight.[5] Threats related to poverty, such as substandard housing, homelessness, lack of prenatal care, and poor nourishment, are identifiable detriments to fetal health, yet there is no public commitment to their eradication. Nor is the harm of burdening women with total responsibility for the nurturance of children and families addressed.

The failure to address this last issue, handing women total responsibility for social reproduction, is the basis of policies that wall in women's reproductive lives. Although the immediate and surface purpose of the reform policies is to save the state from social and fiscal responsibility for vulnerable children and families, there is a deeper purpose based on gender hierarchies.

> The pervasive fear that women will refuse these responsibilities (of social reproduction) is based on the realistic concerns that run deeper than the anxiety that women will "shift" their burden to the state. It has become a full scale fear that women will . . . refuse to play their part in the social arrangements that subordinate women to men, women of color to white women, and single lesbian or bisexual women to women who inhabit normative family configurations.[6]

The crack baby "epidemic," portrayed in news stories of trembling infants, hopelessly damaged by pathologically fiendish mothers, was a public spectacle. Judges, prosecutors, and welfare caseworkers became engaged in a performative process that escalated arrests of mothers.

As more and more mothers were incarcerated, acquiescent public opinion was delivered. The medical establishment produced study after study showing fetal harm but ignored the more accurate studies that indicated that prenatal cocaine exposure causes minor developmental delays.[7]

The point is not that drug use during pregnancy is safe, but that crack babies, identified exclusively with black mothers, became a racial spectacle that punished black women and adversely shaped public opinion. "Although 66.6 percent of crack users are White or Hispanic, defendants convicted of crack cocaine possession in 1994 were 84.5 percent African American."[8] A black mother using drugs during pregnancy is far more likely to lose her baby to the child welfare system than a pregnant white addict. "Between July 1, 1997 and June 30, 2000, DCFS took 39 percent of 5,851 drug-exposed black infants into foster care, versus 27 percent of 1,035 white babies."[9]

No public drama, for example, has focused on the more developmentally damaging harm caused by alcohol use during pregnancy, or on the fact that tobacco smoking correlates with low birth weight and cognitive behavioral problems across race and class lines. A study by the National Institute on Drug Abuse in 1992 indicated that black women drank alcohol during pregnancy at a rate of 16 percent, while white women drank alcohol at a rate of 23 percent.[10] The crack baby epidemic is a racialized and gendered spectacle.

LINDA: "I CAN STILL DANCE"

Linda typifies the crackhead mother. She is black and poor, and she bore drug-addicted babies and used drugs for a number of years before her imprisonment. When we met she was finishing a transition program before returning to her husband and three boys. We spoke after a Christmas party at the program where her boys sat with their father raptly watching their mother and other residents sing "Hark the Herald Angels Sing." Linda is compelling even when she is not on stage. Her lovely face beams with an infectious smile and her black eyes laugh. Beneath her spirited presence is a sadness that she shakes off as if its presence caught her unawares.

What is not typical about Linda's journey is the fact that she has a husband who, with his mother, has cared for his children while his wife was incarcerated. Although only 28 percent of children whose mothers are incarcerated in state prisons remain in their father's care, 90 percent of children are cared for by their mothers during a father's imprisonment.[11]

Linda's life narrative, read from the racialized perspective of the dominant culture, indicts her as a bad mother and her husband as a drug-dealing thug (Tyrone never used drugs, but he has a drug felony conviction for selling). The social gaze that falls upon their lives has a long history. It is a myopic gaze because it cannot or will not see the social scaffolding that holds up their lives for observation, while also holding down their agency. The gaze is blind to the social harms so pervasively subverting Linda and Tyrone's efforts, yet is all encompassing in its surveillance of the family's transgressions.

As a young child Linda learned to tap dance from the best teacher in Chicago, her father Charlie. The Charlie Rogers Dance Studio was open to the neighborhood, but talent, pluck, and flying feet were not enough to feed a family of six children if the flashing feet were black. Linda's pride in her father—"the best tap dancer in the midwest"—was dealt a blow when she was eleven years old and came home to find all of her family's belongings out on the street. That eviction was the beginning of her family's downward slide. As her father's business as a dance teacher declined, the family moved from place to place. Once they were taken in by the Salvation Army. The family ended up in the one place her mother had previously escaped and still hated—the Ida B. Wells housing project.

Maybe my mother's breakdown affected me. She was molested as a child. I was afraid she was crazy, then I was afraid I'd be crazy. My older sister had a nervous breakdown. So I left the house a lot.

That was when I started hanging out with the wrong crowd . . . I dropped out of high school. I wanted money and did not want to be poor. I went to the Audi Home at 14, then to Warrenville for burglary.

Sidewalk high was the school I attended. I went through a lot of pain. I was raped at the age of seventeen and to take away [that pain] I continued to medicate my feelings. I felt everything was someone else's fault but not my own. I continued to go in and out of school. My mother thought I had some problem so I attended family counseling, but no one seemed to understand what I was going through. I strayed from my family.

Linda identifies the desire to dull or obliterate the pain of rape, both her mother's and her own. This experience is all too common for women incarcerated. Beth Ritchie reports that "a survey conducted by the Correctional Association found that over half of all female inmates were victims of physical abuse and thirty-five percent had been victims of sexual abuse"[12] and this figure does not account for rape by strangers. Yet sexual violence against women is accepted as normal or inevitable. There has not been an 800 percent increase in the incarceration of rapists as there has been for the incarceration of black women for nonviolent crimes. In fact "only one in one hundred rapists receives more than a one-year prison sentence for his crime."[13] And rape has increased. The Uniform Crime Report for 1972 to 1991 shows a 128 percent increase in the number of rapes—one rape every five minutes.[14] The state's priorities are not protecting the female body.

Linda doesn't reflect on how the pain of sexual violation affected her youthful sense of self. Researcher Beth Ritchie found that battery or sexual abuse of African-American women so diminished the women's sense of identity and agency as to become a gender cage that encased their spirits.[15] Their humiliation and loss of confidence, coupled with a sense of isolation, amounted to trauma, which, together with poverty, caused them to unravel. Linda watched her own mother break down as a result of sexual violence and the defeat of moving back to the projects.

TAKING OFF THE TAP SHOES

Linda also unraveled at age seventeen. She was already addicted to heroin when she dated Tyrone but she kept it a secret for years. Her addiction lasted seven years. The story of those years frightens her but she insists on telling the truth.

All my children were born addicted. The only reason I got them home from the hospital is because of my mother-in-law and Tyrone or else DCFS would have taken them. . . . I never did the service plan DCFS wanted so they gave temporary custody to my mother-in-law. Eventually DCFS terminated my parental rights. I signed the papers because I had an understanding that I'd have the boys returned to me when I got my life together. I was so hurt when my name was removed from their birth certificates.

Both Tyrone and Linda were better able to support their family by selling drugs than when they both had jobs at a candle factory. When drug money wasn't paying well Tyrone got a job, but Linda was an addict and couldn't hold a job long. Her last baby was born crack addicted. All she could imagine in her future was *boosting* and selling and using. She came back from Dwight Prison and went right back to drugs. When her father was dying she put herself on methadone in order to care for him. She recalls, "Charlie's legs were finally gone. He couldn't talk but I still understood him. The night he died I told my sister I'd get my life together. She didn't believe me."

Somehow Charlie's death rattled Linda's cage of despair and fatalism. She was his spirited tap-dancing child who lost that sense of self, of specialness. She was determined to reinvent her self—not just as Charlie's daughter, Tyrone's wife, or the boys' mother, but as who she was.

The waiting period for entrance to a drug rehab program was two months. Linda was allowed to stay for three months, but she knew it wasn't enough time. She was just beginning to see her addiction as a disease rather than an irredeemable, monstrous character flaw, when she had to leave. After she was incarcerated and preparing to return to her family, a counselor recommended her to Grace House, a transition house that only accepts highly motivated women for a protracted stay. It is not a treatment center; the program's philosophy is to focus on and support women's strengths, and to emphasize the community as a healer.

They accepted me and it was a blessing. The kids wanted me home. So did their dad. But I tried to tell them I was helping not just me but all of us. I started working on me.

[But] I was worried about my kids. They were acting out and seeing a psychologist [apparently at their school]. They wanted to put them on Ritalin, but I told them not to take it. Kids are not supposed to be on Ritalin for long. Tyrone says it makes them too quiet, but their grandma wants them to take it. I try not to think Grandma just wants more money from disability . . . but I have to trust her as their caretaker even if I don't agree with her. We have to come together, to work together.

Linda's choice of a program that allows her to find her lost self is the beginning of her own agency, but even as she struggles to rebuild her shattered life, the surveillance network is regulating and overseeing her family's life. School counselors have classified and medicated her children. Her mother-in-law will receive government benefits because of the children's "disabilities." Linda does not have a legal right to be her children's mother.

Identifying the surveillance process that is already classifying her boys is not meant to deny the effects on her boys of their mother's addiction and imprisonment. Nor is it meant to indict teachers, school psychologists, or caseworkers individually—they too are caught in a process whose various surveillance network's cumulative and encompassing effects eludes them. Linda's middle son was getting As, but when Linda went to prison he failed a grade. Her youngest almost made the honor roll, but he has a nervous condition.

> Linda   The school counselor said my baby was refusing to sit still and he was hitting kids. He would only behave when he could read.

Her oldest boy, JP, is nine. He looks angelic and I comment that JP's demeanor is calm and shy, but his mother says his quiet politeness is misleading.

> Linda   JP is like me. He is the rebel. He has street sense and he knows a lot. I just don't want him to follow me to the streets. I worry. He's seen a psychologist.
>
> JP   I didn't like the psychiatrist because I knew I wasn't crazy.
>
> Linda   JP told the psychologist that a ghost named Mary Adams came out of the mirror. He just did it to mess with him.
>
> JP   (Laughs.)
>
> Linda   JP was fighting all the time and his attention span was too short. Plus he saw everything backwards.
>
> JP   I was stabbing my paper with a pen because I was angry. This boy was talking about me. He said "Yo Mama is a hippie druggie con." He was bigger and we fought. I threw a bottle at his head.

JP and his brothers are all bright and because they attend one of the magnet schools they have received the special attention of school psychologists and counselors. In the non-magnet public schools in their neighborhood, their cases would have received no attention due to lack of resources. Ironically this attention comes from professionals who view the boys as psychically damaged and in need of behavior management. Is the stigma of their mother's imprisonment transferred to them or are the counselors picking up on the effects of the trauma of their mother's incarceration?

What might have been this family's chances if the time and money that has gone into monitoring, disciplining, and classifying them had been spent on services that they, not the state, identified as needed? What if they had had the opportunity for jobs that paid decent wages? Even now, at Linda's turning point, the social inequities that shaped her youth dog her efforts at renewal.

Linda	I've been here for nine months and I'm getting out soon. It's hard to find a place for a family. Even if I don't have custody I want my children to come over. I only make $7.35 per hour working for food service at a college. There's a ten-year waiting list for subsidized housing. Tyrone is not working now.
Tyrone	I've got a forklift license, but I have a felony conviction for selling drugs so it's hard. I need a job I can keep for a long time. Last job was like slavery. I was moving dead cows at Waxler Meat. They weighed 1,400 pounds and I had to move ten trucks a day for $6.50 an hour. It was working in a freezer. I'd have stayed there if I wasn't hassled and told to speed up all the time. Those millionaire owners didn't pay us nothin'.
Linda	I see a better future for my children now that I'm doing better. I try to let Tyrone know it's going to be ok. He doesn't believe me but I want him to know good is going to happen.
Tyrone	Still I think God has somethin' good in store for us. I always been good and I think good comes to good.
Linda	(Laughs) I can still tap dance.

Even as she says this Tyrone frowns. He doesn't really see a way out for them.

FOR EXPENDABLE POPULATIONS ONLY: DRUG, WELFARE, AND REPRODUCTIVE POLICIES

This is not a family that is considered salvageable. Rather than investing in eradicating poverty, government spending on the war to eradicate drugs rose from $200 million in 1970 to $13 billion in 1992. New harsh mandatory minimum sentences include five-year sentences for offenses involving 5 grams of crack cocaine, although the same sentence is given for offenses involving 500 grams of powder cocaine. Powder cocaine is more expensive than crack cocaine, and the majority of powder cocaine users are white. In 1994 those convicted of crack possession were overwhelmingly (84.5 percent) African Americans.[16] In 1986, before mandatory minimum sentences became law, the racial sentencing differential was that blacks received 6 percent longer sentences than whites. Within four years of the enactment, blacks had sentences 93 percent longer than whites.[17]

Poor urban residents who use crack receive sentences 100 times more punitive than those given to more affluent users of powder cocaine. In fact, powder cocaine users caught with exactly the same amount of cocaine as crack users will usually receive probation, while crack users receive five-year prison sentences. "Under this formula a dealer charged with trafficking 400 grams of powder, worth $40,000, could receive a shorter sentence than a user he supplied with crack valued at $500. Crack is the only drug that carries a mandatory prison sentence for first offense possession."[18]

Far from protecting the offspring of drug-using mothers, drug laws have imperiled children. Many pregnant addicts, fearing police reports, avoid seeking prenatal care that could strengthen both mother and child. Many drug treatment centers refuse admittance to pregnant women or they lack facilities for mothers with children. As Linda's story shows, the waiting list for admittance to urban drug rehab programs is long. In addition, Clinton's Welfare Reform Act permits states to deny drug treatment attendance to persons with drug felony convictions. If they do attend rehab programs, the time does not count toward their mandated work hours. Further, persons with drug or alcohol addictions can no longer receive Supplemental Security Income (SSI).

Once again the enactment of racialized spectacle is apparent in the enforcement of reproductive controls. In Chicago, African-American women were "about half as likely to get pre-natal care as white women."[19] A Pinellas County, Florida study found that black women were ten times more likely than white women to be reported to child welfare agencies for drug use during pregnancy.[20] While African-American women have been the primary target population for controlling assistance and neglect by governing bodies, other women of color are also subject to lethal reproductive policies. Puerto Rican and Native American women had alarming sterilization rates throughout the 1970s. Between the 1930s and the 1970s, one third of Puerto Rican women had been sterilized.[21] According to an American Civil Liberties Union report, judges in several states gave women convicted of drug abuse during pregnancy or of child abuse, the choice of using the contraceptive Norplant or going to jail.[22] Norplant, which is implanted in the arm, is effective for five years and has severe side effects.

With respect to women of color, who are not prevented from having children, governing authorities have a feeble to nonexistent commitment to their infant's health and well-being. African-American and Latino mothers lack prenatal care, which leads to low-birth-weight babies. These vulnerable children are categorized as at-risk due to their mothers' "failures" rather than from a lack of public health care clinics, social and health insurance, or available drug treatment programs.

The babies of the expendable are at daily and hourly risk in America. According to the Children's Defense Fund *every day* 751 Latino babies and 514 black babies are born poor, 518 Latino and 216 black babies have no health insurance, 157 Latino and black babies are born with low birth rates, and 24 black and 12 Latino babies die.[23]

A stark and illustrative index of expendability has been welfare reform's restrictions on benefits to children and mothers with disabilities. Four years after welfare reform, "only 29 percent of low income single mothers with disabled children received TANF benefits."[24] An even more critical lifeline for poor mothers who have disabilities or have children with disabilities is SSI, which was also cut. "Among low income single mother families with both mother and child disabled 30 percent received SSI benefits for the child or the mother."[25]

Caseworkers in child welfare bureaucracies, public aid agencies, and health care clinics for the indigent become the disciplinary agents who enforce punitive regulations. The protocols they follow leave little room for creativity or dissent even if they recognize the coercive and degrading nature of the stipulations. The transactions between caseworkers and clients reinforce hierarchies of dominance and subjugation.

Carcel policies further jeopardize the children of poor mothers who have "done their time" According to section 15 of the Welfare Reform Act, any felon convicted of drug-related crimes (the majority of women prisoners) cannot receive government benefits for their families. This is a lifetime ban. A woman could embezzle a million dollars, use or distribute heroin, speed, or other drugs, and still not lose government benefits upon her prison release. Possession of four grams of crack is the one and only crime that will get her cut off welfare forever. This ban affects 135,000 children and in the seven states that have implemented it, the majority of the women affected are African American and Hispanic.[26]

Franciscan Sister Patricia Schlosser, who works as a social worker with Cook County, Illinois mothers transitioning from prison back to family life, summarizes the stigmatizing effects of incarceration:

> I think that their lives are affected forever. Family relationships are damaged, they've virtually lost their parenting role, their authority—parole makes them vulnerable and it's extremely difficult to get a job as a former inmate.[27]

WELFARE REFORM AS A DYNAMIC PROCESS

With the passage of the Personal Responsibility and Work Opportunity Reconciliation Act of 1996, there was not even a mention of creating employment opportunities in spite of the obvious need to absorb masses of new workers. The absence of debate indicated the triumph of the assumption that jobs were available, yet the ongoing process of deindustrialization, which displaced so many workers in manufacturing beginning in the 1970s, left many families with little recourse but to depend on welfare benefits. Clinton's welfare reform is part of a political process, which, like economic policies, has underwritten the creation of the surplus poor.

Dominant control is not achieved exclusively through limiting economic opportunity; it is achieved through political policies, such as welfare legislation and crime bills that maintain a racially stratified social order, which inevitably becomes normalized. The fact that Clinton's Welfare Reform Act aroused little public resistance attests to the acceptance of a lengthy two party assault on public consciousness about the source of social and moral problems in the nation. This victory was only possible through both the vigorous victim blaming of conservatives and the subtle racial policies of liberals who advocated *race-blind* policies that masked the nonwhite policy targets.[28]

The Personal Responsibility and Work Opportunity Reconciliation Act represents the virtually uncontested achievement of white hegemony. Its accomplishment does not represent a new policy shift that abandons the poor as much as it is part of a process of gendered racism that is dynamic, adaptive, and continuous.[29] *Welfare racism* is an ideological/political process of social control of restive populations of color through regulation of the lives of women, especially black women.[30] In the thirty years since Lyndon Johnson's War on Poverty, welfare has become linked to black mothers in spite of the fact that historically poor whites were more highly represented on welfare rolls. Just as incarcerated mothers of color have been stigmatized as monstrous, so too single black mothers on welfare have been cast as promiscuous, indolent baby-making machines living off of the state.

Moral stigmatization of black mothers serves a threefold purpose. It deflects public attention away from gendered racial oppression, justifies regulative policies that punish moral transgressors, and maintains hierarchies of power and privilege. In summary, black women are held responsible for America's most persistent moral problems: They are the producers of poverty, drugs, and crime rather than the victims of gendered racial oppression.

The moral stigmatization of African-American women in welfare discourse and the process of racial control of which it is a component have not come only from those occupying positions in a racial state—from Congressman on down to welfare officials. They have also come from the mass media, policy research and think-tank analysts, university-based social scientists, independent intellectuals and the general public.[31]

Child advocate Valerie Polakow calls welfare reform, and the national failure to provide poor families with decent child care, health insurance, good schools, and safe housing, "savage policies" that amount to a "public assault on children."[32]

OF BODIES AND BONDAGE: A HISTORY
OF EXPENDABILITY

Since the fifteenth century the bodies of the colonized, such as Indian and African slaves in the Americas, have been essential to the building of European power and wealth. The same bodies have been expendable when they are used up or superfluous. Deindustrialization in the globalized economy has created a surplus of postcolonial bodies. These bodies, no longer absorbed in a high-tech, highly skilled workforce, are disciplined through a carcel network that is pervasive and normalized. The carcel network is a prison without walls that exists outside as well as inside the penitentiary. The carcel's disciplinary processes maintain racial, class, and gender hierarchies.

The disciplinary process flows through bureaucracies, policies, laws, and social images that prepare society to accept coercive measures as necessary for the protection of the common good. Surveillance and regulation of the "dangerous" or "helpless" people is possible through controlling images that mark them as outlaws, social cripples, or at-risk populations that need fixing. These *deficient* peoples are drawn from the pool of the unproductive. Thus, surplus people—welfare mothers and their at-risk children, developmentally challenged people, immigrants from the poorer continents, Native Americans on reservations, black and brown peoples concentrated in urban ghettoes—are subjugated through racialized and gendered systems of care and protection, as well as incarcerative justice systems.

The "helpless"—"at risk" and of different abilities—are less vulnerable to paternalistic regulation and protection if they have enough financial support to avoid state assistance. For the impoverished developmentally challenged person, however, there has been the protection of the state. Beginning in the Progressive Era, eugenics policies institutionalized developmentally challenged people who were often subjected to sterilization. For example, in 1975 a North Carolina statute permitted the sterilization of the "mentally defective" (the "feeble-minded," "imbeciles," and "idiots"), who were defined as retarded and lacking self-control and the ability to manage themselves. Permission to sterilize such a person could be given by the superintendent or director of a county institution or social service organization.[33]

No subjugated body has needed oversight as critically as mothers of the colonized whether Puerto Rican, Mexican-American, Native American, or African-American women. Since slavery, black women, portrayed as licentious and degenerate women lacking maternal instincts, have had their children labeled as being at-risk and subsequently subject to social and child welfare policies until their children reach youthful agency when they, too, become social threats. Black women, as the biological and social reproducers of future generations, are portrayed as producers of a violent and degenerate underclass, a recent code word for the racialized poor. Though subject to reproductive control from slave captivity by means of rape, and subsequent legal and economic commodification of their bodies and children's lives, promiscuous unwed mothers or opportunistic welfare queens have been held responsible for America's moral crisis.

While slave masters had the power to compel compliance with their procreative mandates through force, current policies more often achieve their ends through the manipulation of government benefits. While slave owners profited from encouraging slave women to bear many children, modern-day taxpayers believe they save money by discouraging poor black women from having children.[34]

Powerful images of uncaring, parasitic welfare cheats, prostitutes, and drug addicts detract scrutiny from colonial histories, policies, and laws that maintain a racialized system of social inequity. "Facing sexual imperialism that is reminiscent of slavery, African American women often find their bodies are simultaneously reduced to units of labor and sexual commodities."[35]

The increased incarceration of women of color is part of a multilayered process of recolonization that serves the interests of elite managers of a globalized economy, but it also uses addicted mothers of color as spectacle. Christian Parenti argues that the incarceration rage "is at one level a rational strategy for managing the contradictions of a restructured American capitalism . . . but at another level, the big lock-up is merely the useful policy by-product of electoral strategies in which right-wing politicians *use* the theme of crime and punishment to get elected, while masking their all-important pro-business agenda."[36]

6

INCARCERATION: THEATER OF TERROR[1]

[T]he terrors of Gulag America function theatrically, providing spectacles that have a negative impact, first of all, on those marked as poor and racially other. . . . Spectacles of lockdown America involve the sacrifice of so-called surplus populations . . . through isolation of them, rejection, exclusion, para-military police, intimidations and crackdowns, imprisonment and executions.

Mark Lewis Taylor[2]

For incarcerated women, theatrical sites of terror exist both inside and outside the walls of prisons. Women's high incidence (over 50 percent) of physical and sexual abuse prior to incarceration attests to the social terror of their lives outside of prison. Brutal prison conditions often replicate prior abuse, reinventing and reinforcing spectacles of terror within America's gulag.

These spectacles terrorize children, too. Children are affected by the abuse of their parents before arrest (male assault of mothers in 90 percent of the cases), and they are affected by the terrors suffered by their parents in prison. If prisons provided authentic rehabilitation programs with effective family support initiatives, the futures of children and mothers might not appear so uncertain and frightening. For example, if a mother receives drug rehabilitation, job preparation training, an opportunity to complete high school, college, or vocational courses, and if she is able to maintain her bonds with her children, the family's separation is less traumatic and the future holds some promise. But with few notable exceptions, this is not the reality. Instead of mothers finding ways to take positive steps toward change, they find that opportunities are thwarted or haphazardly and feebly presented. These experiences send the clear message that these women and their children do not count in America. This chapter unmasks the terrorizing purposes of the imprisonment of women as spectacle and attempts to understand the reproduction of that terror in their children.

For women outside prison, the theater of terror plays hourly. One researcher reports: "Based on the last 17 years of empirical inquiry, experts now estimate that as many as *4 million women experience severe or life threatening assault from a male partner in an average 12 month period in the United States*; and that *one in every three women* will experience at least one physical assault by an intimate partner during adulthood."[3] Nearly one-half million (409,820) rapes and sexual assaults are committed annually against women. Ninety percent of rape victims are female. A Bureau of Justice Statistics report indicates that most rapes and sexual assaults are not reported to the police.[4]

Violence within the prison walls is also terrifying because there is no place to hide from an abuser. Based on the reports of the Government Accounting Office, Amnesty International and Human Rights Watch, women prisoners are subject to sexual harassment, sexual abuse, and retaliation for reporting abuse, which amounts to terror. According to Human Rights Watch, "Being a woman prisoner in a U.S. state prison can be a terrifying experience."[5]

Social permission for spectacles of violence against women leads society to accept gender roles that are unequal. Alarming statistics of sexual abuse of women has little effect on desensitized social agents who have been disciplined to acceptance by the repetitive occurrences of physical and sexual violence. A 1995 study by the U.S. Department of Justice found that nearly all of the women interviewed in Michigan prisons said they had experienced sexual harassment or aggression by male guards, including improper visual surveillance, fondling, and rape.[6] After the U.S. Justice Department joined Human Rights Watch's class action suit against the Michigan Department of Corrections in 1997, a campaign of revenge began. All the women who brought complaints of sexual aggression and assault suffered retaliation by correctional personnel, who denied the women privileges and wrote fraudulent disciplinary *tickets*, which caused some women to lose "good" time.[7] A 1996 Human Rights Watch Report found widespread patterns of sexual abuse in its study of five state prisons for women in California, Georgia, Illinois, Michigan, and New York as well as in the District of Columbia.[8]

When the female subjects of violence are black, racialized images normalize or erase the occurrence. Black women's bodies have borne not only the slave master's lash, but insidious images of hypersexuality that deflect notice of their rape. Social violence against black women evokes little response. Similarly, Native American women, Latinas, and poor white women's sexual and physical abuse or violation registers little public outcry. The fact that 60 percent of women in state prisons reported experiences of physical or sexual abuse prior to incarceration[9] is simply seen as part of the pathologies that surround their violent existences. Governing authorities do not notice the causal links between years of physical or sexual terror and subsequent drug use.

Two discourses on women are rarely linked at a strategic policy level—the discourse on women criminals and the discourse on violence against women. The discourse on violence against women has not decreased practices of battery and rape, but the discourse on female criminality has shaped an exponential increase in incarceration of women. Policy makers do not make connections between these discourses and practices because to do so would place women's social location within a context of permissive violence and terror. Repetitive, daily terror of women continues because of feeble sanctions against male violence, and it creates despair among already socially powerless women. This in turn leads some to drug use, and in the minds of governing bodies, justifies their incarceration. These women are considered disposable, and so are their children.

THEY COULDN'T MAKE ME SHUT UP

The trauma of physical or sexual violence shuts up children, and too often, shuts them down as adult women. Rosé Lopez never did shut up. The terror of her childhood abuse was reprised when she was incarcerated for a drug offense, but she resisted for nine years in a New Mexico prison.

I spent two years in the hole because I wouldn't break. I held my own. Whenever something went down—a woman got raped, I called my Mom who spread the word. They had a Supermax (super maximum prison) where they put me.

I wasn't gang affiliated so they couldn't get me for selling drugs. Nothing they could do . . . I wouldn't shut up!

Placing women in segregation for reporting sexual assault is not an uncommon practice. According to Human Rights Watch,

> Grievance or investigatory procedures, where they exist, are often ineffectual, and corrections employees continue to engage in abuse because they believe they will rarely be held accountable, administratively, civilly, or criminally. Few people outside the prison walls know what is going on or care if they do know.[10]

One can only imagine the courage required to confront sexual assault when it is clear that society has averted its gaze and retaliation is assured. Yet many women, like Rosé, came forward in California, Illinois, Michigan, New York, and the District of Columbia to lodge complaints of sexual aggression or assault knowing that when the researchers left (even when the researchers were from the U.S. Department of Justice) they would be targeted for retaliation. These resistances write subversive scripts against the drama of terror. They disrupt, but don't end, the spectacle of terror. These practices are deeply embedded in processes of social control—so much so that even judicial orders are defied. Entire prison systems openly defy class action suit stipulations and/or federal investigations. When the U.S Department of Justice began investigating complaints of sexual abuse in Michigan prisons, the Michigan Department of Corrections initially refused to allow federal investigators into the prisons![11]

Rosé's own experience of powerlessness caused her to develop rage and despair that almost killed her, but also gave her a sense of solidarity with those brutalized by bullies. She does not think of her own actions as courageous—they are simply what integrity demanded of her. Currently Rosé works as a reintegration specialist for former drug felon Latinas, and as a researcher with an Albuquerque community-based family reunification program. She deeply understands the link between family terror of women and girls and their turning to drugs for relief or out of despair.

I started glue sniffing at nine. My father was the meanest person I ever met. He was a Golden Gloves boxer in the Air Force—a raging alcoholic, who beat my mother terribly. I can remember being in the bathtub and seeing the welts on my legs from his beatings. I would do things to distract me from the beatings of my mom . . . glue sniffing or I stole beer.

My brother who was thirteen raped me continually beginning when I was nine. My mom was brainwashed by my dad. I never told her what my brother did because I was afraid it would cause problems. I knew I wasn't valued. My brother had been raping me and I knew I didn't matter to anyone. I was very angry. I would hit myself in the face out of rage.

I did heroin at sixteen. It was sweet; everything went away. Then if there was a drug, I'd do it. I always wanted to go right to the edge of death and stay there. My little brother found me almost dead in the bathroom. He saved my life.

I had no faith in myself, but my cousins' faith in me gave me a hope I'd never had. I couldn't understand how they could love me. They wanted more from me than I thought I had. So [when I left prison] I went to anger management classes and to therapy. Then I went to Community College. I even snuck into classes at University of New Mexico to learn how to argue. I loved school.

Rosé is forty years old and she has found a home at Peanut Butter and Jelly, one of the few comprehensive, not-for-profit programs for former prisoners and their children. From her perspective, the prison system's major purposes—suppression of dissent, punishment of victims, and making money from women's incarceration—duplicate the terror of her family.

Prison is a pimp because it makes money off people's difficulties. The war on drugs is a war on the poor—a way to make money warehousing people and making sure they come back again.

Rosé still won't shut up.

I don't know how to stay down. I want to work for my people. I want the poor, the Latinos in the South Valley, to have a chance. I want to apply the same tenacity I learned in the streets to hit legislators. If one person stays out of prison, that's my revenge. I used to say I do this work for revenge because so many cops beat me up in prison. Now I do it for justice.

"SO MANY COPS BEAT ME UP IN PRISON"

International conventions prohibit cruel, inhumane, or torturous acts against prisoners, yet the United States, as signatory to both the International Covenant on Civil and Political Rights (ICCPR) and the International Convention against Torture and Other Cruel, Inhumane, and Degrading Treatment or Punishment, allows sexual torture in its prisons. The ICCPR upholds a prisoner's right to privacy—a right violated by the common practice of strip searches of U.S. women inmates by male officers.[12] In fact, the United Nations Minimum Rules for the Treatment of Prisoners forbids guards of the opposite sex to function in correctional roles.[13] The United States as a signatory to international human rights treaties under the ICCPR, as well as the Convention on the Elimination of All Forms of Racial Discrimination (CERD) and the Convention against Torture (CAT), is *four years overdue* in reporting to CERD remedies for its failure to protect women from abuse, lack of adequate health care, and racially discriminatory sentencing penalties.[14]

Many women who were victims of sexual abuse prior to entering prisons are retraumatized either through further victimization or because they are terrorized into silence by witnessing spectacles of sexual assault. The theater of sexual terror teaches women to shut up and take orders lest they suffer the fate of resisters like Rosé. Human Rights Watch reports that "for women with or without a history of abuse, to be punished for reporting the abuse is to be made acutely aware of one's powerlessness and vulnerability." Several of the women interviewed by Human Rights Watch investigators suffered serious psychological harm as a result of having been abused in prison.[15]

In 2001 and 2002, story after story of sexual abuse of youth by clerics poured forth in the media, and the public was educated about some of the links between sexual abuse, powerlessness, and posttraumatic stress syndrome in later life. The *teachers* were men in their thirties and forties who were finally believed after twenty or thirty years of social disbelief and cover-up by Catholic authorities. Over and over, male victims of clerical sexual assault told of adult lives of addiction, depression, attempted suicide, debilitating shame, and rage. Few blamed the victims for their maladaptive behaviors, but the situation has been different for female felons with drug-related offenses, who often are blamed for their own suffering. Women prisoners are raped or know of assaults on others, and they either remain silenced and traumatized or they speak out and face retaliation. When women are released from prison, society is shocked when they relapse into drug use or other illegal activities. If they are mothers, the scorn intensifies. Their children bear the stigma, and they too internalize society's standards, and come to consider their convicted mothers to be bad.

Although many state prison systems for women, including Michigan, have stated policies of zero tolerance for sexual misconduct on the part of guards, they function much like archdiocesan systems, which used secrecy and cover-up before the public outcry against clerical pedophilia. After the U.S. Department of Justice's class action suit against the Michigan Department of Corrections for failure to protect women from the sexual misconduct of male guards, prison administrators agreed to prohibit male guards from patrolling female inmates' housing units. However, the prohibitions applied to only 250 of the 10,000 positions held by correctional officers, and of those 250 jobs, only 50 to 100 were held by males.[16]

THE OTHER SHOE: THE PRISON LITIGATION REFORM ACT OF 1996

Reforms serve the interests of the powerful by deflecting public scrutiny from the failure of public institutions, and more precisely, from charges of inhumane treatment. Government reforms have cut off social spending as part of a neoliberal economic policy that has served the interests of an international corporate sector by eliminating government benefits to populations that are no longer valuable as sources of cheap, unskilled labor.

Prior to 1996, the single most critical legal protection for incarcerated women was the advocacy of private attorneys and a few national organizations that challenged sexual misconduct by prison employees. But President Clinton's 1996 Prison Litigation Reform Act (PLRA) limited the ability of individual attorneys and not-for-profit organizations to use litigation as a strategy for addressing and curtailing the abuse of women prisoners. The PLRA prohibits litigation that lacks a finding that the conditions in question violate the U.S. Constitution or a federal statute. In addition, the PLRA restricts court-appointed lawyers' fees. According to Human Rights Watch, "The passage of the PLRA removes the one effective external check on serious abuse. . . . the United States has almost completely abdicated its responsibility to guarantee in any meaningful way that women held in its state prisons are not being sexually abused by those in authority over them."[17]

As part of the privatization of services occurring as the government abandons support for poor and vulnerable groups, privatized transportation of prisoners has been contracted to for-profit corporations. But the same male violence that infests the state prison systems continues in the private sector. Robin Darbyshire barely escaped rape and murder at the hands of an employee of Extraditions International, a private prisoner transport company. During the four-day transport from Nevada to a Colorado jail, she was sexually harassed and abused, and the 325-pound guard threatened to shoot her for attempted escape if she screamed. In addition to filing suit against Extraditions International, the American Civil Liberties Union has filed suit against another for-profit transport company, Transcor, for charges of sexual abuse against women prisoners.[18]

JUST DON'T GET SICK IN PRISON AND DON'T BE PREGNANT!

Up to 10 percent of women entering prisons are pregnant.[19] The mothers give birth in hospitals, and often many arrive in shackles. Amnesty International found that some are actually shackled during labor or following birth.[20] The majority of these women are nonviolent felons. These widespread practices inscribed on the confined bodies of mothers and newborns brand both mother and child as outlaws. Almost 1,000 babies were born to incarcerated mothers in 1996. With the exception of a few maternal-infant care centers, almost all of those babies spent no more than several hours with their mothers in prison.[21]

The depression following separation that affects both the mother and baby remains invisible. Who can bear to examine such suffering? Almost everyone looks away, either to protect themselves from the anguish of knowing, or because they do not believe unfit mothers deserve their children. These mothers grieve, as do the mothers whose parental rights are terminated. Mothers whose children are placed in adoptive homes or foster care often become depressed. In a study of mothers in a Montana prison, the researcher found that Native American mothers from tribal lands whose children were placed with extended family members experienced far less anxiety and depression than landless Native American mothers who lacked a community of support and whose children were placed in the foster homes of strangers. One participant, whose children were placed in an adoptive home, never saw them again and she "grieved for them as though they were dead."[22]

Joanne Archibald, Program Director at Chicago Legal Advocacy for Incarcerated Mothers, was separated from her infant son when she spent a year and a half in prison on a drug charge. The baby was eighteen months old when she left. He was placed in the care of a loving friend, but the effects of that separation were enormous. Her boy spent years in therapy, speaking of suicide in spite of his mother's constant support and assurance that she would never again abandon him. Throughout his childhood, her son was a high academic achiever and was highly regarded by his teachers, but the wound of abandonment was carried into his growing years. Only the immense devotion of his mother and the teachers and therapist from whom she sought help on his behalf were able to assist him in recovering from the trauma of his mother's absence when he was eighteen months old.

Prenatal care varies from prison to prison with some mothers-to-be virtually begging for care. The powerlessness of these mothers all but obliterates their sense of agency. They are at the mercy of the state when their children are born and before their birth. To be at the mercy of prison health care systems can be life threatening.

According to Dr. Gwendolyn Dennard, the chief medical officer at the Central California Women's Facility in Chowchilla, California, forty-four-year-old heart patient Susan Bouchard died because of inadequate physician and nursing care in that prison.[23] Susan had sought medical help for chest pains for three days but the doctor never came. When her heart attack began, her cellmates called for help, but a hospital was not called for another thirty minutes. By the time the ambulance arrived Susan was dead.[24]

The Central California Women's Facility at Chowchilla's skilled nursing facility is infamous for its callousness. If the bodies of young women in prison are considered disposable, the bodies of the old or critically ill are considered absolutely worthless. Chowchilla is the end of the line—a place in the desert where torture under the guise of medical care has continued in spite of public protests. If you file an appeal against the staff, it will take a year to be reviewed. And you can count on retaliation in the form of reduced care, which, if you are diabetic or wheelchair confined or dependent on timely administration of medicines, can be life threatening. The message is to die quietly.

In January 2002 a class action suit was brought against the California Department of Corrections (DOC), which charged the DOC with indifference to patients' health care. What led to the suit's filing was a previous suit filed against the skilled nursing facility at Chowchilla as a result of a mysterious rash of nine deaths in just eight weeks. In addition, Chowchilla had received citation after citation based on investigations by state-appointed evaluators. Nevertheless, the women's skilled nursing facility at Chowchilla was not specifically singled out in the suit.

Other states are subject to class action suits for violation of women's rights. One of the more infamous women's prisons, besides Chowchilla, is located in Alabama. Due to overcrowding, the situation in Tutwiler Women's Prison in Alabama was so volatile that U.S. District Court Judge Myron Thompson ordered state officials to change the conditions. The prison's maximum capacity of 417 has grown to over 1,000 inmates. While Chowchilla was charged with lethal indifference to the bodies of the sick, Tutwiler was charged with indifferently packing the bodies of healthy black women into spaces reminiscent of the holds of slaver ships.

Amnesty International found that in 1996 not even half (47 percent) of women entering prison received a medical health evaluation, and in 1994 only half received mammograms or pap smears.[25] Inadequate mental health care and overmedication of women with psychotropic drugs is common. Between 48 and 88 percent of women inmates have suffered prior sexual or physical abuse, but very few receive counseling for this trauma once they are incarcerated.[26] These are the bodies made into spectacle and made disposable.

CHILDREN AS AUDIENCE IN THE THEATER OF TERROR

The theater of terror profoundly affects the children of incarcerated mothers. They have been the terrified audience, as well as the players. The terror of their mother's leaving and imprisonment marks them deeply. Caretakers try to blunt the fear they carry, but the children know that each time they pass through a prison gate, each time they are patted down, their bodies and their people's bodies are marked for surveillance. They cannot escape it. They either tremble before the terror or defy it, making its magnitude and danger smaller by growing indifferent to its fierceness. The children who understand the spectacle's terrorizing purpose, and imagine a human drama in which they count, transform the terror. But such transformation demands resistance, communities of hope, and advocates who love these children intensely.

Most children are pummeled by the war on drugs. Like soldiers who have seen too much death, children internalize the terror of their parents' imprisonment. The fear of it can silence them, immobilize them, or enrage them. The pain they carry is invisible, but if it displays itself in illegal behavior when they are adults, they will be criminalized, institutionalized, or even killed. The theater of terror is reproduced in the children of the incarcerated.

7

TEEN MOTHERS AND THE INFANTS
WHO SAVED THEM

I wondered where children got their strength.

James Baldwin[1]

Yolanda and Ann both spent time in Albuquerque New Mexico's Youth Diagnostic and Development Center (YDDC) for incarcerated teens. YDDC has a program that allows teen mothers to spend a couple of afternoons or evenings a week with their babies. I visited there twice. It is a program kinder than many, but it is heart wrenching to see fifteen-year-olds clinging to their infants, walking them along the tiled institutional floors, cooing, rocking, and handing rattles and pacifiers to the tiny bundled infants they carry for two precious hours. Most of them, children themselves, take parenting classes to gain clues about the roles that fate and their own longings have called them to early. Some are too wounded to take in much. Others grasp whatever keys to parenting they are offered. Few had role models they want to emulate. They have to learn, at fifteen or sixteen, how to come to grips with the anguish they carry, and to love another more than their own drama.

What's remarkable is the human capacity to give love in spite of histories of abuse and sometimes torture. Often someone such as an aunt or older sibling has parented the abused child, offering enough nurturance that they find some courage to love. This was true for Yolanda.

Yolanda's newly discovered sense of worth is transforming her sense of possibility. When we meet, Yolanda cradles her baby, Maria Patricia, whispering, "*Mi amor, mi amor*" (my love, my love). Yolanda has a scar on her cinnamon forehead and I wonder if it is from a beating. The young mother is beautiful and her gaze is direct. There is a bewildered look about her as if she is still surprised at the support she's received. Two University of New Mexico law students have taken her case and they keep asking her to come to the university campus, trying to edge her toward taking a course, to fulfill her dream to be a social worker; someone who can, at least, put their finger in the dyke to hold back the flood that threatens so many like her.

The support of these law students has sparked Yolanda's initiative, but her deep sense of purpose has come from her baby girl. Yolanda has become fierce in her determination to protect her child from the brutality she's experienced. Her need to protect her baby echoes the love of the only person who protected her throughout her childhood—her sister.

At ten years old things went bad for me. I had a best friend Elizabeth and her father molested me. He left a hickey on my neck and my Mom saw it. I always got beat, so I was scared. I didn't know what a hickey was. My Mom hit me with a belt buckle and she was so enraged that she hit me until I was bleeding. I was numb. My mom went to his house but she didn't press charges. I was hurt that she didn't press charges. I felt so angry at my mother. My sister had left for the army and she was my angel—my everything. I had to sleep alone after my sister left and I was afraid. So I asked my Mom if I could sleep with her, but she said no.

But she let my male cousin sleep in the room with me. He was feeling me every night. But I was lucky he didn't rape me. Then my other cousin slept with me. I was afraid to tell my mom who'd beat me. I built up so much hate that I fought all the time. I started ditching school in fifth grade. By middle school I was in trouble with the cops for graffiti. Then I kicked a gang girl in the face. I was fighting everywhere. Girls would talk smack to me and I'd fight. I ran away from home. I got assault and battery charges. Finally, I got a year at YDDC. When I was on restricted probation I got pregnant. But the baby's father, Luis, beat me and I was so weak that the baby died after I gave birth to her.

But I ran away again with Luis—the guy who beat me. I went to school and was doing good but he started beating me up again during my [next] pregnancy. They [police] picked me up again at school.

The rage that has burned up Yolanda's path and incinerated her self-possession seems quieted by Maria Patricia's presence and law students who affirm her intelligence and determination. The law students have helped her discover an intense sense of justice beneath the anger. Hannah Arendt once said, "Rage is by no means an automatic reaction to misery and suffering . . . only where conditions could be changed and are not does rage arise."[2]

Yolanda says she'll never go near Luis again. She and Maria Patricia stand a chance now because her spirit has been revivified and she's discovered a *chispa* (spark) of goodness and spunk beneath her anger. But the world does not seem to believe in her. She's branded. Those law students will have to stay close so that the snares of exclusion—when she is blocked from decent paying jobs, or she can't manage to take advantage of courses at the University of New Mexico along with parenting and work—don't overwhelm her.

Yolanda will be confronted with the social inequities that confront young, poor, single parent Latinas, but at least she doesn't have to beat an addiction also. In that she's unique. Too many female addicts are victims of abuse who gamble with the destruction of drugs, abandoning friends and children because of poisonous self-hatred. To refuse such branding is not simply an act of self-redemption, it is a social and political act of cultural resistance. It tears away the power of familial fists, social stigmas, and punitive institutional practices, and shreds the message that young women are nothing but receptacles for sexual use. It is an act of faith that not everyone can muster. Sometimes it takes years to make. Sister Kathy Nolan of Grace House believes that her one task is to help women believe in their own capacity for love.

> Most of my work is to help women believe they are lovable, to trust their own goodness. The ones who can't believe that go back to drugs. These women feel they are throwaway people. Society sends [wounded] people back to the same neighborhoods and we guarantee they'll go back to drugs and prison . . . unless they die.[3]

For Kathy Nolan, accompanying women who return from prison is a journey through rage and justice, and love and death. Because she is a nun, perhaps it is not surprising that love and justice are part of the equation, but rage and death are not so expected. Nolan's rage is the flip side of her love. She must temper it every time she hears the stories of the sexual violence and vicious beatings that tortured these women when they were younger, and that ripped away their faith in themselves and others. She must temper it when she sees these women being punished further by the state. This book is about survivors but Kathy

Nolan wants a book about those victims of violence who couldn't make it—the women who died in a back alley from an overdose, those beaten to death by a pimp, and those who took their own lives.

These victims' stories are rarely told, and if told, few can see the depths of suffering and even resistance that women whose lives were taken by themselves or others muster. Poet June Jordan's own mother's suicide may have been her last act of resistance against the "deaths" that stalked her:

> [a] death you cannot possibly pinpoint because she died so many, many times and, because even before she became your mother, the life of that woman was taken. . . . I came too late to help my mother to her feet. By way of everlasting thanks to all of the women who have helped me to stay alive, I am working never to be late again.[4]

The stakes are love or death. Those stakes are never more stark than for those working with adolescent women who are or have been incarcerated. Ironically, those young women who have only begun to experience the punishment of the streets and prisons are more walled away from love than seasoned women who have walked into the infernos of drugs, pimps, and prisons for years. Author bell hooks says,

> Young people are cynical about love. Ultimately, cynicism is the great mask of the disappointed and betrayed heart. . . . To them, love is for the naive, the weak, the hopelessly romantic. . . . Everyday thousands of children in our culture are verbally, and physically abused, starved, tortured and murdered . . . victims of intimate terrorism in that they have no collective voice or rights. . . . Only love can heal the wounds of the past.[5]

Ms. hook's emphasis on love as transfomative, and as a critical beginning for the recovery of self-respect, does not overlook the systemic hatred, neglect, and abuse perpetuated by racism and social inequality. Over and over again she emphasizes that there can be no love without justice.

Young women in youth detention centers bring the despair of family betrayal to the houses and courts of justice, where they experience more blame and become more cynical. Their own confusion and immaturity leads them to throw up a wall against those who genuinely want to help. But the helpers—caseworkers and corrections counselors—represent a punitive system. Stubbornly, often to their own detriment, young women resist, trusting an intuitive sense of the injustice that masquerades as justice. Ann's life is an example of that injustice and of how easy it is to go to jail.

Ann, who is Cherokee and Caucasian, is a new mother who was confined to the YDDC in Albuquerque because, she says, she resisted leaving her hometown in Iowa and came to New Mexico. All of her trouble started when her single-parent mother brought her to Tucumcari, New Mexico, to live with an aunt.

I got into a fight with my aunt who was drunk and cussing me out—I beat her up. She called the cops and I was taken to a detention center and released, but I was put on two years probation so I couldn't leave New Mexico for two years. I was a straight-A student until I came to high school in New Mexico. I violated probation because school was boring and I wanted advanced classes. I refused to go to school. A warrant was issued for my arrest, so I ran. I moved in with my child's father who was thirty-eight. I was fourteen.

I went back to my aunt's after seven months because I was scared and I turned myself in. I knew I'd go to jail because my mom was working at a factory that made motor parts for an Air Force base and she couldn't afford to pay for a lawyer. I was sent to a residential treatment center. Then I got two years in a New Mexico Girls School for not going to school! After I got out of the treatment center, I moved back in with my boyfriend and became pregnant with my son. But my partner, who did drugs, beat me up so bad that I miscarried. I was always the target of his violent rages. Then I got pregnant with my daughter, but I was more scared to leave him than to stay with him.

Then I was arrested for breaking probation because I left the state with my partner to go to Texas for a year. When they found out where I was they expedited me back to New Mexico and I was sentenced [to YDDC] for two years.

None of the staff there wanted me to keep my baby. Her father didn't want her because he was afraid they'd arrest him for statutory rape of a sixteen-year-old. I didn't press charges because it was consensual. They put my baby in foster care and the state thought I'd give up fighting for my baby. They tried to prove me an unfit mother because I came from an unstable environment. It broke my heart when they took my baby from me—it's a mother's worst nightmare.

She was afraid initially to ask her mother to take the baby because they clearly were angry at each other. Ann says her mother wasn't ready to be a mom.

She tried her best but she couldn't make good decisions. She didn't stop me from being with my partner even though he was hurting me. I think my mom felt powerless and she just gave up.

Ann outsmarted the caseworkers and kept her child, or at least she thinks she did. For the eight months that her daughter was in foster care while Ann was in YDDC, she was permitted to see her baby sporadically. Fearing she'd lose custody because the foster family wanted to adopt the baby, she managed to get legal guardianship papers and fill them out, giving custody to an aunt and uncle back in Iowa. She tricked her caseworker into sending her to get something notarized. The notary apparently didn't pay attention to the papers she was imprinting with the notary seal.

It isn't clear if Ann was the clever one or her caseworker looked the other way. What is clear is Ann's intelligence. She's received her GED and took two courses at the community college while incarcerated. When she was in Texas (after she ran away from her mother and aunt) she worked as a loan officer while still sixteen. She's participated in a program that unites moms and babies, teaches parenting classes, and helps young women examine the reasons they stayed with abusive men.

My self-worth was zero when I went to YDDC. I didn't believe I should be on the face of the Earth. I was on a path of death. I wasn't suicidal but I was tired of the abuse—of being put down—so I was angry at everyone. When I didn't care about my life anymore I used crack because he was a dealer. I'd never used before that.

I'm going back to the Midwest with my baby. I'd like to go to a community college. Everything I do now affects my little girl. Everything changes when you bring a child into the world. I fought tooth and nail for my daughter. It's my daughter that kept me going.

What seems to have *saved* Ann and Yolanda more than anyone or anything else was their children's births and their own motherhood. For young people taught that they count for nothing, a baby's utter need and radical claim on love can teach them something new and precious about who they are. But little in society will support them. Programs that simply stress that young women don't deserve to be abused and that they should be good parents and not abuse their children are not enough. Such programs skirt the continued social abuse they will receive. They focus on the young women's abusive families, which is crucial, but they rarely focus on a social system that is as abusive as the families and partners who have hurt them.

BREAKING THE COLONIZING MENTALITIES' IMAGES OF SHAME AND SUBORDINATION

Rage directed at oppressive and inequitable conditions can be creative and even salvific. Programs need to confront not just abuse and internalized oppression, but also the ways in which minds and hearts become colonized. The colonized mentality keeps many women locked in cells of fear and self-loathing where abuse is accepted as deserved, long after the women have been released from prison. "It is this kind of colonized behavior that is often attributed to abused children and especially battered women, who are so often not only physically but also mentally tortured so that their perspective on the world becomes that of the colonizers in regard to themselves."[6]

Racism beats down the spirit and rapes the soul. The self-hatred of these terrorized young women is intensified by a country that claims to be color neutral, yet systematically but subtly discriminates against people of color. Without politicizing programs, young women can't escape the mentality of the colonizing culture, because they can't identify the social and continually reconfigured sources of race, sex, and class subordination. Moreover, domesticated or bureaucratized programs are political processes that avoid confronting systems of domination and subordination. Such programs may unwittingly encourage young women to be more feminine and more successful, reinforcing patterns of oppression—seeking male approval for their sense of identity, stepping on others to get ahead, attaching their worth to things or looks, consuming in order to feel valuable—all legal activities encouraged by the dominant culture.

Most insidious of all the colonizer's myths, and that which particularly affects young women, is the myth of the willing victim. Few of these young women appear victimized because they have toughened up to survive, but most blame themselves for the beatings and abuse they've endured. Without politicizing programs and exposing the truth about inequities of class, race, and sexual power, it is impossible to dispel that myth. If they only learn to recognize the injustice of an individual abuser, they will remain vulnerable to the various interrelated forms of social abuse they encounter daily. To discover the social sources of injustice is liberating because it breaks the hold of the colonizing mentality and invites the young person into solidarity with others who suffer and resist. That solidarity leads to a sense of purpose and dignity, and a growing sense of self-control that anger management training can't produce.

One hardly expects that correctional departments will produce such programs. Yet even outside agencies fear politicizing their programs. The colonizing mentalities, which shape drug policy and its correctional and rehabilitative programs, regard male drug use as illegal but not as pathological. Girls who use drugs, however,

> are figured as out of control, promiscuous, emotionally disturbed, psychopathological. Deviant behavior in women is always gender deviance, perennially raising questions about women's gender performance and their moral and psychological fitness for motherhood. . . . Women who use drugs were and are construed as "monsters," especially when they are unwilling or unable to meet "their" responsibilities for social reproduction.[7]

These images have the power to discipline women in institutions of punishment and in the outside world. Young women need to uncover the ways in which they were disciplined by family terror and punished by incarceration, and they will continue to be disciplined to their gender, class, and racial roles when they leave youth jails or prisons. Moreover, they need, in the words of bell hooks, to discover their marginal position as a place of resistance, a place where their confused and rebellious instincts are not punished but understood. "Understanding marginality as a position and place of resistance is crucial for the oppressed, exploited, marginalized people. If we only view the margin as a sign marking despair, a deep nihilism penetrates . . . these margins have been both sites of repression and sites of resistance."[8]

There is a current emphasis on *restorative justice programs*, which have probably saved some young lives from entering the criminal justice system. Restorative justice programs have been instrumental in setting up prison and jail diversion programs in poor communities. Young people meet their victims and are ordered to make some kind of restitution to the individual and community through service or repayment. *Drug courts,* which are community based, have kept many young people from prison, but these programs are small and sporadic. Moreover, restorative justice does not restore to the offender the justice of lives devoid of terror, poverty, and social exclusion. We do not need more programs to change these young people's lives, but rather programs to change an oppressive social order.

8

CHILDREN IN THE OTHER AMERICA

Acknowledging the scandalous conditions of those who live in poverty often requires a rejection of comfortable relativism.

Paul Farmer, M.D.[1]

In a culture of domination everyone is socialized to accept violence as an acceptable means of social control.

bell hooks[2]

Like most Americans, the children of imprisoned mothers accept social violence as normal, and it is their bodies that are imprinted with its daily bruises. Perhaps what is most damaging to the children of imprisoned mothers is the child's inchoate sense that the social violence layered onto their lives is the fault of their parents, their race, their gender. Mothers, who themselves have lived through similar childhoods, must somehow hold back a culture that tells children that the very things that make them who they are, are somehow flawed. A child cannot discern the grand social context of his or her family's suffering. Families may break or fight the onslaught that confronts them daily, but either way, the children will interpret their triumph or failure within the framework they have been given. Social success, or the abject failure that a mother's imprisonment represents, is seen as a matter of individual choice. The social causes that overwhelm vulnerable families often remain invisible to mothers, children, and the society that holds them accountable for their difficulties.

Most of the mothers I interviewed for this book blamed themselves for their addiction, imprisonment, and abandonment of their children. While the need to take responsibility for one's actions is essential to recovery from addiction or self-destructive behavior, the macro-level inequities that shape these women's lives and identities remain hidden, thus normalizing women's experiences of social, economic, and political subjugation. Take, for example, Janelle. Unlike most mothers who fear their children will be taken by child welfare authorities because of their incarceration or addiction, Janelle voluntarily gave them up to save them from herself.

My second daughter Mildred was born addicted, and when I saw that baby go through tremors, it devastated me. But I tried to hold on because I loved them but what life could I give? When Ralph was born I called DCFS, and by July of 1989 I signed over my rights to him. I was tired of hurting my children. I sat down my eleven-year-old and told her I needed help and that I was giving her to my mother. I gave Joe, my ex-husband, the two youngest boys. I was so devastated that I went back to drugs.

I had no excuse for leaving the kids alone, for not changing diapers . . . I gave them up to make them happy. I've written a letter to each of them asking to be a part of their lives. [Tears are streaming down her face] I just wish there were a way to reverse the termination of parental rights but there isn't . . . Joe is a good man and I think he is right to keep the children away from me because I always disappointed them. I had no excuse for not changing diapers, for leaving the children alone. I'm learning to overcome negativity.

Janelle knows the negativity is generational. Her mother, also a single parent, was an alcoholic who, in Janelle's words, "was never there for me, so I thought I was an ugly duckling." Janelle was drinking when she was nine years old, and the sister who raised her introduced her to drugs when she was twelve. She dropped out of high school in her junior year because she was using drugs. All six of her siblings were addicted to drugs. Janelle clearly understands that her dysfunctional addictive family shaped her own addiction, incarceration, and loss of her children. She accepts as normal her family's poverty, inferior schooling, a racially segregated neighborhood where drug selling is the most profitable venue in the community. Janelle accepts as "normal" the incarceration of most of the young men in her neighborhood including all of her brothers. Even if she avoids the negativity of her addicted family when she is released from prison, how will she escape the negativity of social exclusion, isolation, and poverty, or the racial and gender stigmas that hold her exclusively responsible for her failure as a mother? "I thought I was a monster," she says.

Janelle blames herself for her maternal failure, which she believes was her responsibility *alone*, thus legitimating gendered expectations of social reproduction. As Nancy Campbell writes,

> Holding individuals responsible for addiction reproduces deeply held American notions of personal responsibility, risk, vulnerability and productive citizenship. But not all individuals have the means or capacities to discharge the responsibilities of citizenship and social reproduction. The uneven distribution of the means to realize autonomy, reduce vulnerability and violence, and carry out responsibilities is simply disregarded in drug policy.[3]

Understanding of both a mother's imprisonment and her children's plight demands an examination of the negative reality that families face daily in the "other America."[4] Children of poor, single mothers of color experience violence that is pervasive and daily.

CHILDREN IN THE OTHER AMERICA

Child Development scholar James Garbarino considers the social world inhabited by poor children to be "socially toxic."[5] Children can absorb some social poisons, but when the deprivations and violence are too thick, most lose resilience regardless of family resistance and effort. Losing a mother to imprisonment for four years (an average for drug-related crimes) is a deprivation that overstresses most children's ability to move through their formative years undamaged. This is not due simply to the loss of their mother at a critical developmental time, but to the other toxicities that have accumulated. According to Garbarino, "They include community violence, child abuse, domestic violence, family disruption, poverty, despair, depression, rejection, paranoia, alienation and other social pollutants that demoralize families and divide communities. These forces contaminate the social environment of children and youth and are the primary elements of social toxicity."[6] These toxicities pervade the social order, but their most dangerous levels occur in the communities of families who have few resources to counteract the danger. The damaging effects of class, race, and gender disparities are concentrated in communities that lack political and economic power, yet the dominant society locates the source of these problems in individual responsibility, thus ignoring lethal social toxicity and blaming the individual families of poor single mothers of color.

The feminization of poverty predicted twenty years ago has galloped into the center ring, yet we barely see the winner. At some time in their childhood, one out of two children will live with a single parent, the vast majority of whom are women.[7] In the year 2000, almost 40 percent (39.8 percent) of the children living in families headed by single women were poor, while only 8.2 percent of children in married families were poor.[8] Rather than focus on the social and economic disparities that penalize single mothers, President Bush supported economic welfare incentives for poor single women who marry. For President Bush, the problem of poverty and racist exclusion will be solved if the single mother marries, but according to researcher Beth Ritchie, it is violently abusive marriages that have led women into prison.[9] The percentage of mothers in prison for killing abusers is small, but the number of women incarcerated after turning to drugs to dull the pain of abuse and subsequent despair is considerable. Almost 60 percent of women in state prisons have experienced some form of physical or sexual abuse, although this number does not differentiate spousal abuse from childhood abuse.[10]

CHILD POVERTY AND VIOLENCE

Poverty is a form of structural violence. Since President Lyndon Johnson's 1964 War on Poverty, millions more people live in poverty while a small percentage of Americans have increased their wealth by billions. The richest 1.5 percent of Americans has amassed nearly half (48 percent) of the nation's financial wealth.[11] By 1983 child poverty had increased by 50 percent,[12] and it continues to climb and to affect the working poor. In 2000 child poverty had risen 37 percent among full-time working families.[13] More than half of poor families experience lack of food, poor housing conditions, utility shutoffs, and the lack of even a stove or refrigerator. One out of six American children are poor in the country with the greatest number of millionaires/billionaires and the highest Gross Domestic Product of any nation in the world.[14]

While the Clinton administration accelerated child poverty by the passage of welfare "reform," the Bush administration's tax cut plan passed in June 2001 will, in ten years, accelerate that trend. Economists speculate that the Bush tax plan will increase the wealth of one percent of the American population to $475 billion, an aggregate greater than the wealth of the lowest 20 percent of the U.S. population.[15] According to Marian Wright Edelman, the director of the Children's Defense

Fund, "the half-a-trillion dollars in tax cuts slated to go to the richest one percent of tax payers is the biggest obstacle to helping poor children."[16]

As more and more wealth moves upward through tax benefits for the rich and elimination of social spending and privatization of social services, the lives of poor children seem to become more and more expendable. For example, compared with other industrialized nations, America's treatment of vulnerable children indicates its irresponsibility. America ranks in the bottom third of industrialized nations that proactively attempt to decrease child poverty, to extend health care insurance for children, or to alter low birth weight of newborns.[17] Only two nations in the world have failed to ratify the United Nations Convention on the Rights of the Child: Somalia, which is not a legal government, and the United States.

Poverty is violent. Policy makers justify punitive responses to mothers who give birth to crack babies, yet there is no outrage over the danger that a newborn faces if his or her mother is impoverished. "A baby born to a poor mother is more likely to die before its first birthday than a baby born to an unwed mother, a high school drop-out, or a mother who smoked during pregnancy, according to the Centers for Disease Control."[18]

> [C]rack is a small and recent addition to an old story. The conditions of poverty—poor nutrition, shoddy housing, vulnerability to disease and stress—threaten the healthy development of a fetus. Babies born into poverty (half of whom are Black children) are also more susceptible to deadly diseases such as influenza and pneumonia. . . . Poverty—not maternal drug use—is the major threat to the health of Black children in America.[19]

Children living in impoverished neighborhoods are far more subject to illness, not because of parental neglect, but because they incur preventable illnesses related to poverty. Escalating cases of lead poisoning, tuberculosis, and asthma afflict children in environments where parents cannot afford to renovate a toxic building, move to an area with cleaner air, or persuade besieged principals of deteriorating public schools to clean up lead paint conditions. According to the Centers for Disease Control and Prevention, children of color up to the age of five years have a 10.5 to 12 times higher incidence of tuberculosis than white children, and 5- to 14-year-old nonwhite children are 19 to 32 times more likely to be infected than whites.[20]

Lead poisoning is associated with brain damage, convulsions, impaired learning abilities, and developmental losses. As Sue Brooks writes,

> Children literally are gasping for their lives, suffering irrevocable damage to their brains and nervous systems, dying painfully and young from the ravages of tuberculosis. . . . Poor children of color, already suffering disproportionately in so many other ways, also are bearing the brunt of environmentally induced damage. . . . As a society we know how to control asthma, know how to eradicate lead poisoning, and know how to prevent tuberculosis, and we are well aware of environmental racism. . . . Reluctance to respond directly . . . to environmentally induced damage reflects judgments of worth [whose health is worth protecting?] bound up in the social values and political struggles of our times.[21]

These violations of children's rights, produced daily and hourly, are a result of unjust and lethal structures. Every minute of every day in America a baby is born without health insurance.[22] This structural inequality also produces direct violence against children. According to the Children's Defense Fund, a ten-year-old American child is at greater risk of violence than a police officer on duty. Every two hours and forty minutes a child or youth is killed by gunfire in armed America.[23]

This violence, which affects children, results from systemic economic disparity, from policies that privilege the wealthy while shredding social spending on welfare, mental health services, drug treatment centers, child care, and decent health care for children.

TAKING OFF THE GLOVES: THE PERSONAL RESPONSIBILITY AND WORK OPPORTUNITY RECONCILIATION ACT OF 1996

The effects on children of President Clinton's passage of the Personal Responsibility and Work Opportunity Reconciliation Act of 1996, which ended welfare as we know it, has amounted to an abdication of social protections for the most vulnerable. Four years after welfare reform was passed, "the proportion of quite poor and extremely poor children whose single parent worked at least some of the time increased significantly—from 50 to 60 percent for quite poor children and 21 to 30 percent for extremely poor children . . . the hardest hit have been those already facing the greatest risk—children younger than six years of age."[24]

Both the cutoff of all public assistance to families after five years and a projected mandatory forty-hour workweek for single mothers of children over the age of one has created a national child care crisis, particularly for infant and toddler care. Single mothers on workfare cannot afford the high cost of quality child care and are forced to place young children in poor-quality day care centers. The result of welfare reform is predictable: The children of poor parents will be ill prepared to succeed in school. A 1999 study has shown that privileged children in good-quality day care had greater math and thinking skills and fewer behavioral problems than children in low cost, low-quality day care who enter kindergarten already behind in academic skills.[25]

Head Start, the one effective preparatory program for the children of the poor, only serves 50 percent of eligible children. Almost 7 million children are left home alone each week![26] By 2003, President Bush suggested a need to reform the Head Start program. Even for the 15 million children eligible for Head Start assistance only 12 percent receive that benefit.[27] Imagine a system capable of monitoring every single mother who must work 30 to 40 hours per week to receive welfare benefits, but that cannot provide child care assistance to 78 percent of the eligible children. If the Department of Children and Family Services discovers that a child has been left home alone while the mother works, the child may be removed from the mother and placed under state care. When the millions of children who had poor-quality day care (or none at all) enter kindergarten already ill prepared, their lack of academic success is blamed not on the real sources of the problem, but on their single mother's moral failure.

Four years after President Clinton's slicing of the already fraying net of social benefits, the welfare rolls have dropped massively—but is that success? Mandated work has not lifted children's families out of poverty. Without child care or a high school diploma, it is close to impossible for a single mother to hold a decent paying job. In 2000, in spite of parental employment, 58 percent of low-income families still lived below the poverty line, with more than 50 percent of these parents unable to pay rent, buy food, or afford medical care.[28]

These social impediments to child and family security make up the structure of a social system that not only fails to prevent poverty but perpetuates it. The social costs of poverty are great: increased numbers of families living in shelters, exponential incarceration of mothers for drug-related economic crimes, increased hospitalizations particularly for asthmatic children, more need for special education classes, increased criminal justice spending, the need for food pantries and soup kitchens, increased family violence, and more children in foster care. While some argue that the business sector benefits from welfare reform because it offers up a new source of cheap labor, the costs to the state of creating surplus populations are greater. Why does this continue when the social costs of poverty are so large?

SOCIAL CONTROL THROUGH GENDERED RACISM

Inexpensive female labor, made available through mandatory workfare, does not explain the fiscal drain represented by increasing poverty. A social will to eliminate poverty would require building inclusive economic structures that offer opportunity to all citizens. The impediment to such a commitment is a legacy of racialized political and economic policies that systemically exclude people of color.

> Establishing structures of economic opportunity for people of color would entail more than competent schools, career training, available employment, child care, and job referrals. It would require opening up the entire labor market, which is now so geographically and occupationally stratified by race and class that poor communities are confined to only a tiny fraction of job opportunities. It would include a commitment to all remaining forms of racial exclusion.[29]

By the end of the 1960s, the Civil Rights Movement threatened to create such equity by demanding not just an end to Jim Crow segregation but also economic parity with whites. Welfare and children's rights activists and prison reform activists made advances in the brief political space opened at the end of the 1960s and early 1970s, but white backlash, fanned by "controlling images"[30] of violent black men and sassy, undeserving welfare mothers, created a climate for punitive policies. By the 1980s, President Reagan began a racialized war on drugs that criminalized African-American males, exploded prison construction, and established a permanent state of mass incarceration.[31]

> A complex set of social and political developments have produced a wave of building and filling prisons that is virtually unprecedented in human history. Beginning with a prison population of just under 200,000 in 1972, the number of inmates in United States prisons has increased to . . . 1.2 million by 1997.[32]

During the 1980s, socially excluded black youth, immoral welfare-dependent unwed mothers, and superpredatory males were portrayed as the source of violence in America. These stigmatized and outlawed young people became the clients of expanded incarceration and a devolved welfare system in the 1990s. They were held responsible for exclusionary racial and gender policies created to maintain a system of white privilege.

RACIALIZED IMMIGRATION POLICIES AND PRACTICES

In the last twenty years, racialized immigration policies have sought to control U.S. borders by excluding refugees from the third and fourth worlds. People fleeing persecution to the safety of the land of the free have been treated as criminals. According to Amnesty International, people seeking political asylum have been incarcerated, "stripped and searched; shackled and chained; sometimes verbally or physically abused. . . . The INS (Immigration and Naturalization Service) relies heavily on standards produced by the American Correctional Association (ACA) for holding prisoners, standards inappropriate for refugees."[33]

By the late 1990s, and before September 11, 2001, the numbers of people detained by the INS had increased 75 percent, although lack of data makes it impossible to know how many sought political asylum or how many were undocumented.[34] Fifty percent of detainees are held in jails where they do not have the rights of prisoners tried and sentenced by the U.S. justice system. Unlike sentenced U.S. inmates, asylum seekers, most of whom do not speak English, may or may not have the right to counsel, they may or may not be allowed family visits, and they have no idea when they will be released. However, they do receive treatment similar to prisoners, including body searches and spending time in solitary confinement.[35]

Somalian refugee Hawa Abdi Jama describes spending hours in a large overcrowded room in a New Jersey detention center where he became sick: "I asked for some water. Then the guard grabbed my hair and kicked me in the stomach and on the legs and on the head. After she beat me, they took me to the isolation room for a day and a half."[36]

Children are also held in detention centers, often separated from their parents for months. They are treated as illegal aliens and thus criminalized. Some teenage refugees who have fled violence in their home countries are held in juvenile correctional centers. The majority of these children have come from Africa, Latin America, or Asia.

If a refugee family does make it through INS, the possibility of receiving government benefits has been virtually eliminated by provisions in Clinton's welfare reform act. The provision that refuses TANF benefits to illegal aliens and curtails eligibility to legal aliens for five years is an immigration disincentive to refugees. "The racial actors who framed the immigration provisions of the PRWORA [Personal Responsibility and Work Opportunity Reconciliation Act of 1996] treated certain immigrant groups as foreign 'aliens' who threatened to undermine core U.S. values of 'self-sufficiency.'"[37]

Welfare reform, drug laws, and immigration reform are policies that control and contain specific racial bodies. Reforms of policies targeting people of color respond to surges at our borders, uprisings, or social campaigns within our borders. In addition, reform policies specifically affecting women (primarily women of color) respond to the historical dynamics of poor women's reproductive needs. Thus, although my research has situated racist policies against children in the context of structural economic violence, these gendered and racialized policies are part of a dynamic historical process equally as determinantal. Cazenave and Neubeck locate gendered racism as both a system and an ongoing process of social control.[38] The goal of such a process is racial containment and control of the reproductive lives of women of color.

These processes are produced by, and in turn reproduce, moral images that justify shifting policies and laws to control nonwhite bodies, especially reproductive bodies. Long before poor women of color end up in prison, they are sentenced to a moral judgment that classifies them as unfit mothers. Continually besieged by state scrutiny through affiliations with public aid, public hospitals, immigration agents, and child welfare agencies, their agency for their families is not judged sufficient. Racialized welfare and immigration policies, discriminatory drug laws, and punitive child welfare policies are rationalized as means of protecting children from irresponsible women. Yet the stigmas that brand mothers morally unfit also brand their children. Unlike Christian stigmatics whose bodies bore open, bleeding wounds, these children carry invisible wounds inscribed at birth on their black, brown, and red bodies. These are bodies more vulnerable to illness, violence, and incarceration. The lives of the children of the other America bleed away; only their mothers and fathers witness it. America's governing body averts its gaze from their pain, while assuring their containment through the scrutinizing gaze of public institutions.

GULAG NATION

The children of the other America live in the catchment areas from which potential convicts will be selected. The dominant culture portrays these zones of urban ghettoes, barrios, reservations, and impoverished ethnic enclaves as locations of, and producers of, violence. But in fact, the other America is the recipient of massive, explosive forms of social attack and punishment, which amounts, in Dorothy Robert's analysis, to a policy of "killing the black body."[39] Of the two million incarcerated people in the United States, 50 percent are African American and sixteen percent are Latino.[40] Michel Foucault described incarceration as the preeminent means of disciplining bodies and maintaining social control. The effects of incarceration are felt throughout America's social body with stigmatized children marked as *other*. They carry on their bodies disciplinary wounds of a carcel network, whether they become homeless, hospitalized for preventable illnesses, clients of jail, detention, or zero tolerance expulsion programs, runaways from sexual or physical abuse, or whether they are institutionalized in the child welfare system.[41] The existence of this socially pervasive carcel network disciplines all bodies, both the well fed and well housed, as well as the institutionalized poor and the stigmatized. The reality of institutionalized punishment and state execution forewarns all. For Foucault, the carcel network is total in its social discipline. No body is free. Young males of color overwhelmingly constitute the gulag's populace. Women's bodies are disciplined through coercive reproductive policies from lack of prenatal health care, to serialization, to enforced heterosexist standards of sexuality and family life.

The bodies subject to the most intrusive discipline are nonwhite. The passage of the Homeland Security Act of 2002 and the increased border surveillance of the 1990s led to an explosion of male immigrant detainees. One of Clinton's welfare reform objectives was to create a disincentive for immigrants seeking welfare benefits in the United States. By tying TANF benefits to residency and citizenship, immigrant mothers and children lost meager welfare benefits.[42] As Mark Harris Taylor explains,

> Society exercises this discipline not only in its punitive institutions such as prisons, but also in pre-schools, and other educational institutions, in the workplace, on sidewalks and highways, through social mores about sexuality and marriage, in medical institutions, insurance provisioning, through repeated exposure to mass media images, in organizations for the mentally ill, and so on. All these make up an elaborate network that shapes and disciplines bodies and their everyday performance.[43]

Situated within a process of vertical wealth transfer, accelerated by President Bush's tax cut plan, are policies that enforce a disciplinary carcel network: (1) the incarceration binge of the last twenty years; (2) President Reagan's shredding of the safety net for welfare recipients; (3) President Clinton's scissoring of the remains of social welfare; and (4) President Bush's tax cut plan. The bodies that absorb the effects of these policies are mothers and children. Teens of color endure stepped-up surveillance, which transfers convicted adolescents to adult prisons. Their mothers endure enforced welfare requirements that maintain poverty wages, and more and more are incarcerated for committing economic nonviolent crime.

Disciplinary processes maintain power inequities through institutions of daily control. These racialized and gendered processes and policies determine life chances: which children will flourish or die; which adolescents will go to college or go to prison; and which mothers will be able to feed, clothe, shelter, and protect their children from the social violence of preventable illnesses, inferior education, street violence, incarceration, addiction, or despair.

The children of prisoners confront a daily narrative that incriminates them and face "savage inequalities" that mark them.[44] Author bell hooks reminds us that in a culture dominated by race, gender, and class hierarchies, violence against the subjugated and their children is "normal."

9

GONNA RISE: PAM'S STORY

Have you ever been in a storm with nowhere to run, nowhere to hide? I'm speaking about a storm where you throw your hands up over your head and fall to your knees right where you're standing.

Pam Thomas[1]

The night I began this chapter on the life of Pam Thomas—former addict, convicted felon, and mother of three—I received a call from my sister telling me she'd have to pick me up early from the retreat center where I was writing because, as regional director of a Wisconsin child welfare agency, she had an emergency. She had to tell a depressed and isolated mother that her only son had been found by his foster parents hanging in a closet. I was confronted with the mystery of human suffering. I was as confounded by a thirteen-year-old boy's despair at the world as I was surprised by six-year-old Pam Thomas's childish choice to live in spite of rape and abandonment. By all logic, Pam Thomas could have been a suicide too, but the body that was marked for disposability survived. Pam refused to embrace the death of hope.

Pam is an artist—a poet, dancer, and actress. When I first saw Pam she was on stage performing in a community theater with a group of former prisoners in a drama about their lives called *Only Women Bleed*. Pam's gaze is intense and unafraid, but her presence is almost shy. Her chocolate face, thin as an El Greco figure, is lovely. She moves with the fluidity of a dancer, her long fingers signifying and musical. There is a force to her presence—not from projection of personality, but the opposite. She is held back, her poetry and reflections somehow intensified by the lean, untheatrical economy of her speech. She is a natural performer—laid back, minimal, yet vivid—and you can't take your eyes off her.

Besides writing and acting in plays that tell the story of the incarceration of women in America, Pam has written a training manual for women leaving prison. Her salaried job was as a client services manager at a North Lawndale employment center, where she specialized in helping former prisoners find work. She's on a mission to keep others from a journey like her own. Pam's workbook addresses issues of self-respect and worthlessness because she knows the women have "thrown themselves away" as so much "social junk" (to use a phrase coined by criminologist Steve Spritzer).[2] Step by step, Pam calls the women to reclaim themselves from the social refuse pile, where they have been heaped and forgotten.

But the workbook is not simply spiritual and psychological advice from someone one who has been there. It is also a social indictment. If the women must face their demons and take responsibility for the suffering they've caused, especially to their children, America, too, must face its crimes against the poor. In one of Pam's poems she cops to her failures, but also addresses an unnamed terror.

> Yeah, you got me real good with those poppy seeds and cocoa plants.
> My love for them was a hard as your love for me when I came to your prisons
> and did your free labor.
> You think I don't see you got that ace up your sleeve, your fingers on the rope pulling the noose so tight I can't breathe.[3]

Pam knows the stigma that she and her sisters must confront. The black female body is marked—a life sentence of racial and sexual subordination. Nevertheless, Pam throws up subversive hope.

> Yeah, I know you've branded me for life.
> I get reminded every time I go fill out a job application . . .
> I get reminded every time I go through a door and it gets shut in my face, like when I applied for a student loan.
> I get reminded when I see the faces of my children I didn't raise.
> Yeah I know I played my part, that I don't deny, but you played yours too.
> I get reminded every time I see a new prison go up.
> I know you're waiting for me to slip, so you can get a grip

and give me the taste of a different whip.
I know you're waiting on my children but you can't have them . . .
It's not too late even with this X on my back.[4]

Pam Thomas offers her sisters performative speech intended to awaken their agency and to unmask the theater of terror that swept them up and swept them away. Pam is an actress in what Mark Lewis Taylor calls the theater of counterterror.[5] In the theater of counterterror, dramatic action is used as "bodily contestation and as a creative enactment of new worlds."[6]

Today, I have new dreams.
Keep your minimum wage jobs and your phony apologies
because today I know how to make my own doors
instead of wasting time trying to get through yours . . .
I will not let this X hold me back.
Today I am somebody who knows the truth.
I am what you locked up and tried to keep hidden.
I am a community.[7]

The essence of the theater of counterterror is expressed in Pam's final line—neither she nor her sisters are alone. If abuse and terror have isolated them, if Gulag America has branded them for life, and if their own weakness has shamed them, then their power is found precisely in that vulnerability, and in their refusal to be expendable, alone, and without voice. "I am a community" is a dangerous memory for the great-grandchildren of slaves, who took lash, leg irons, and loss of children, but who held to the beloved community. Pam's communal affiliation is a discourse that undermines the terror of the X that inscribes incarcerated bodies. Pam's is a theatricality that trumps the despair of individualism. Mark Taylor sees rebellious art as both an imaginative act of resistance and a utopian map that envisions change and locates a shift in current reality:

Rebellious art has the fruit of building collective force that can rival otherwise overwhelming oppressive force. . . . Creative expressions anticipate future worlds often so effectively that these worlds are made present before their realization. . . . Amid the terrors of lockdown America, especially, despairing cynicism will always be near at hand. We will need drama and dancing more than ever, to help us envision the future we dream of but cannot see on the horizons of our history.[8]

TOXIC REMEDY FOR A TOXIC CHILDHOOD

be careful of the wolf in sheep's clothing.
If I'd of known that stuff was toxic.
If I'd of known it was going to be my breakfast, lunch, dinner,
my lover, my life, I'd of still done the same thing
because it was too late by then.[9]

Pam Thomas's single-parent mother had nine children. It's not clear to Pam when her mother's drinking started, only that by the time Pam was seven, she became the backbone of the family. Her mother was never home.

I took on the mother role and never had a childhood. I got beat a lot because I took up for my brothers. From the time I was six or maybe I was seven or eight, I was sexually molested. My mother used to send us to a neighborhood church each week, just to give her space away. The minister there sexually molested me . . . it went on for a long time until a neighbor called DCFS. They came and asked my mother about this, but I wouldn't tell because I knew if I did I'd be sent away and my brothers would be left unprotected. But I was sent to my father's in Indiana for two weeks. That's when my baby sister was killed. She was only two years old, but she wandered into the street at 2 A.M. looking for me, and she was killed by a car. I never did tell my father about how that baby died, and I never told him about my molestation. My brothers and I have secrets still.

When Pam was eleven, her mother threw her out of the house. When the police found her wandering the streets without a coat in winter they took her home. Her mother told them she was a run-away and that they should put her in juvenile detention. Somehow they released her, but from then on she was on the streets. But this time she knew how to avoid the police. She made a bed of old coats in a boxcar and slept there. For food money she did sexual favors for men in the area. What follows is one instance of the kindness of strangers that still stays with Pam: "There was a woman in a restaurant who brought me in and fed me, night after night. I never paid her. I still don't know what happened to that woman."

She lived like that for over four years. When she was sixteen she met a thirty-five-year-old truck driver who took her in. At least she was warm and fed, but he wouldn't allow her to leave the apartment when he was on his runs.

He had two Doberman Pinchers who snarled if I went near the door. I had my first child by him, but I left before I had my baby. After that I started tooting powder cocaine. My addict friends taught me how to boost clothes to pay for my habit.

Pam was arrested the first time when she was twenty years old and pregnant. They gave her probation, but she never went to see her probation officer, so she got six months. She went to jail after she had the baby.

One day they came into my cell and told me to come with them to the hospital. My baby had died of crib death. I had to see that little body lying on a gurney. After that I shut down. I didn't care about anything. I went down. [Later] I started smoking crack.

The next time she was arrested she was sent downstate to Logan Prison in 1993. She tried to get drug treatment but it was only available for men at the time. From there she went back and forth between Dixon, Logan, and boot camp, and finally to Dwight Women's Prison.

At Dwight I had a "red badge," which means "high risk," because I'd violated my parole. I saw young women come in and be put on psychotropic drugs. What kept me sane was my children. I still didn't understand my addiction. I had to research what it does to the body on my own. At first I thought all my problems were because of something in me, but then I started to look at society for the first time. And I started to listen to the women and the stories of their lives.

Pam was beginning to identify the social patterns that affected the lives of the women to whom she was listening, but it wasn't until she took action that things fell into place. Brazilian educator Paulo Freire has said that action accelerates and confirms critical awareness. It is the rebellious act against injustice, not prior knowledge, which opens up awareness. Similarly, Camus believed that true understanding of injustice is known after rebellion.[10] Pam's willingness to risk action was a hunch that exemplified Freire's revolutionary pedagogy, which insists that all true knowledge is discovered as we act to change limiting situations.

I was in solitary a lot. They said I was starting riots. But I just started a newsletter of poetry and opinions because we had nothing. We made eyeglasses for the prison, but none of us could afford to buy them, and I told the other women we were being used. Once I spent sixty days in segregation because I started a petition complaining about the kind of soap we were given. It was so bad our skin was like alligator skin. This was why I was considered an agitator.

I watched the news and observed politics and everything started to fall into place. I saw mothers come into prison with minor cases, and I couldn't understand this, but I began to question. I saw women commit suicide. One OD'd on heroin, and we knew none of us gave it to her so it had to be a guard.

The spectacle of solitary punishment no longer had a coercive, disciplining power.

I challenged that male guards at Dwight would come into our areas unannounced even when we were changing clothes. I got written up. I got used to being disciplined.

There is no rehabilitation. My parole officer asked me if I was rehabilitated. I laughed. I had to fight for a year to be put into college classes. I was lucky to get into horticultural classes.

Pam developed a visceral sense of what is meant by the metaphor of warehousing prisoners.

You just see this long line at intake of young women or you look behind you in the cafeteria and see hundreds of women standing waiting and you wonder what is happening to their kids. The worst was seeing the pregnant women trying to get extra food because they were hungry. They'd stick an apple or piece of bread between their legs. But they were always searched and caught, and then they'd be given disciplinary tickets. It's just sad.

The warehouse metaphor is apt because even as the number of women prisoners increases, Pam sees rehabilitation programs diminishing.

There are no [rehab] programs. Even Gateway [a drug rehabilitation program contracted by the state] went from three buildings down to one. And as for transition programs . . . the only one I'd trust is Grace House because none of the women can afford to pay for residential treatment. We have no jobs, no housing, but Grace House takes us in.

It is in the emptiness of prison life and the way it bears down upon its human occupants that Pam is able to see her own life in a new way. She began to see her failures as connected to the failures of others. Once the social dimension of these women's failures was revealed, Pam asked, "Why?" Why were so many from the same impoverished neighborhoods? Why so many blacks and Puerto Ricans? Why had so many come to prison already victimized physically or sexually? Why were these lives so invisible? As Pam saw her links to others, her compassion and her sense of outrage grew. Once she began to resist unjust treatment, she linked the rules of confined warehousing to the rules of racialized social containment and gendered social control that shaped her life outside prison. Finally she understood the social lessons of confinement and containment.

You are taught to be nothin'. It's not just what your family does. It's environment, it's even school. I carry a. lot of responsibility for my actions but not all of it. The addict/criminal in me is really the result of so much trouble.

I don't want to sound conceited, but I think I'm a good, beautiful person. If I grew up in a middle-class household and my mother, who drank because she couldn't cope with [poverty, single parenthood] had resources, maybe she could have given us a safer life. Who might I have become if my life were safe?

Each woman who resists the verdict that renders them useless and hopeless engages in an act of imagination that subverts spectacles of punishment, which teach them "to be nothin'." Throwing prisoners into solitary for standing up to injustice is a tactic in a theater of suppression. Sometimes it terrorizes women into silence, but from time to time women like Josefina or Pam steal the show. They *win* because they take back power and exercise some control over their seemingly abject, powerless positions. They will not shut up, and disciplinary action loses its power. Their actions reveal the theater of terror. Mark Lewis Taylor reminds us that there are still risks: "In doing so, they face terror, absorb it in their bodies, as it were, even while resisting it."[11]

PAM'S CHILDREN: ABSORBING PAIN

The person who took in Pam's children when she was incarcerated was the mother whose own addiction had led her to abandon Pam and her siblings. Pam's awakening allowed her to see her own mother's addiction and pain in the context of a history of social abuse, and not only as a result of personal failure.

I reached to cover my pain, my mother's pain, her mother's pain. Years on top of years of struggle . . . generations of bitterness twisting and turning inside my soul, wishing to be numb, wishing I could get a grip and a little control.[12]

When Pam went to prison, her oldest and youngest daughters were awarded to her mother, and DCFS terminated her parental rights. Her thirteen-year-old son went with his father in Tennessee where his grades, which were As, dropped to Cs. Since her release she's brought him back to Chicago on visits to connect with his sisters and grandmother. Less anxious, he is again getting As in school. Her youngest daughter, who has been raised by her brother and mother, refuses to recognize Pam as her mother. Pam has respected the child's relationship with the one constant in her life—her grandmother. She goes to their home after school each day and does homework with her daughter, whose grades are slowly improving. The ten-year-old called her Mom last summer for the first time.

But the oldest daughter, who felt Pam's addiction was a betrayal of love, is the one who by all logic should be unreachable. She was the one upon whom all responsibility fell. Yet Pam found a way back to her daughter, who, though she is a seventeen-year-old, single-parent high school dropout, has a mother on her side at last. Perhaps Pam's own forgiveness of her mother, who couldn't cope, affected her daughter.

Pam's forgiveness of her mother is one of the gifts of her discovery of the toxic forces that press down upon generations of women caught in poisoned environments. Pam sat with her daughter and asked her forgiveness for her abandonment. She also shared what she had learned about the way drugs can ravage a heart and mind in the same the way that disease can take over a person until an antidote can stop it. The antidote, Pam explained, is not simply will power, but an awakening that allows a person to confront the shame that has eaten away at dignity and worth. Pam was determined that her daughter would not blame herself for her mother's failure, as she had done. She wanted her daughter to know that the bridge she walked to take back her life terrified her. She had to confront her fears, her shame, and the stigmas that marked her life as wasted. Mostly, Pam wanted her daughter to resist the poisonous social messages that blare at her daily.

Pam's daughter wrote a poignant reflection that describes the pain of her childhood, the anguish of not getting along with her grandmother, and the conviction a child carries that she is unlovable because of her mother's abandonment. It is also a love letter that testifies to the human capacity to transform suffering.

When my mother was in prison I felt alone. My grandmother and I weren't getting along at all. I felt like the only reason she was keeping me was because she had to, not because she loved me and wanted to. She used to tell me that my mom didn't want me, and if she did she wouldn't have given me away. I was told I was stupid and couldn't do anything right.

The caretaker of someone else's children, whether a relative or not, is in a continual struggle to win the child's affection. She may disapprove of a child's tendency to valorize a parent who has failed, and who has placed responsibility on the caretaker. It is a rare person who can handle the child's displaced anger or withdrawal. The child's need to valorize the parent appears to be fantasy or denial, and the caretaker wants to set the record straight, which undermines the mother's relationship and doesn't help the children. Yet these tensions are common.

After a while, I started to wonder why [my mom] did give me away and why my dad didn't take me. I felt like she didn't care about me because that's what I was told. I cried a lot, and I remember wishing she would come and just take me away. I kept all my feelings bottled up inside, and I didn't talk to anybody about what was going on . . . I hated my life because all I got was put-downs. I used to write poems about my mom asking her if she loved me why wouldn't she stop using drugs and be with her kids. I used to cry on my birthdays because she never was there . . . I used to pray she would get better and my life would change. I remember thinking, why does she keep doing the same thing over and over again? I couldn't understand, all I knew is that she said she loved us but then she kept hurting us. When she was clean I knew she cared, but I thought she didn't want us, if she did it would all stop.

The logic of a child is impeccable in its microfocus. What addicted mother interrogated by that logic can possibly face the shame? The way to healing is not through shame, although one's failure must be faced. The spiritual strength needed to resist one's destruction derives from squarely facing the truth, and the truth is larger than family dynamics. The mother must discover the macroschematic affecting her addiction. She must locate her own "downfall" within the context of oppression that has held down generations of her people and her gender. Marilyn Frye uses the metaphor of a birdcage to explain the way we are enculturated to see only aspects of oppression, without seeing the way different forms of subjugation and mistreatment are connected. To only see one wire of the birdcage is to fail to see its confining structure.

It is now possible to grasp one of the reasons why oppression can be hard to see and recognize: one can study the elements of an oppressive structure . . . without seeing the structure as a whole, and hence without seeing or being able to understand that one is looking at a cage and that there are people there who are caged, whose motion and mobility are restricted, whose lives are shaped and reduced.[13]

Pam's seventeen-year-old daughter has just begun the discovery that took her mother years of pain to achieve. Pam has told her daughter that she has faced herself and found a beautiful person and that her child must affirm her own beauty. This "yes" to beauty demands a "no" to social mutilation and annihilation. For bell hooks, the black female must face herself and realize "all that she must struggle against to achieve self-actualization. She must counter the representation of herself, her body, her being as expendable."[14]

As Pam's relationship with her daughter deepened, she was able to talk her into completing high school. Now Pam baby-sits her grandchild while her daughter attends classes at Lake County Community College, where she is studying in hopes of becoming an obstetrician. "My son and daughter call me every day. I never thought it would be possible to bond with my children."

It is the best she can do, but it is not enough. It will never make up for their lost childhoods and their loss of each other, each living separate lives. Pam's daughter recognizes the loss. "I still wish she had been there when I was little so that I could have known that she loved me and she wouldn't hurt me on purpose . . . I really needed her to be there when I was down and hurt."

Yet it is a miracle that this family is rebuilding its bonds of love.

Now that [my mom] is here I know that she cared. Now I can talk to her when I have a problem and I know I will always have somewhere to go. I know now that I have her and that is never going to change because I love her, and now I know that she will always love me no matter what changes we both go through.

THEATER OF THE OPPRESSED

One of Pam Thomas's dreams is to have the play she's written about being in prison produced for community groups. The play—featuring four former prisoners talking, praying, and singing about prison, children, stigma, sorrow, and sassiness—is accompanied by a jazz singer and pianist. It is community theater as much because it is unpolished and raw, as because it, perhaps naively, takes the audience seriously and treats the audience as if it possessed moral spirit and moral power. How often does American theater do that?

Pam's play is an act of resistance that subverts the theatrics of terror, which the incarceration system represents. Unlike spectacles of terror, the theater of the oppressed (a term used by Augusto Boal, who uses theater as fellow Brazilian educator Paulo Freire used critical education) seeks to wake us up to the ways in which our consciousness has been captured and disciplined.[15] Pam's drama gives voice to those who are silenced, reversing the delegitimation of their knowledge and transforming the audience's shallow or captive knowledge. The discourse on prison's purposes, on punishment, rehabilitation, and criminals is reframed, and the boundaries between felons and law-abiding citizens gets blurred and complicated. Audiences are disturbed by suspicions that we are all disciplined to a *normalcy*, and that those who lack the social power to achieve normalcy become social outcasts. Although the playwright's intention is not political, the discourse disrupts the audience's comfort. The presence of former felons speaking of their anguish as mothers complicates moral categories. Of course the degree of confusion or dislocation of assumptions shifts, depending upon the racial and class composition of the community where the play is performed.

At a minimum, such cultural work opens a space for questioning. The question-and-answer period after Pam's play creates a discourse that is rare in America—people asking the players about the meaning of their worlds, and their ideas about prisons, crime, and culpability. There seems to be no question too naive for the women on stage. They are open and accepting, even when the questions are paternalistically racist or sexist. It is clear they intend to be good teachers, aiming to enlighten rather than to reprimand. They relish being the experts, reversing the worthlessness that prison life engenders. Their expertise is legitimated, not by the audience, but by their own history. It is an expertise hard won, and few in the audience can claim it. Those in the audience who have been there join in with the other experts in explaining to the audience the troubled waters in which they've waded.

This theater of the oppressed is an act of faith in the audience, hoping for a communion of attentiveness and solidarity, if only for a few hours. In that limited and vulnerable space, the sites of acceptable terror are interrogated by a community of solidarity, breaking open the disciplinary boundaries that coerce our acceptance of the theater of terror that plays daily, invisibly, and with little contestation.

10

EYE ON THE PRIZE: THEORIZING CHANGE

Racialized socioeconomic patterns are camouflaged by representational practices that criminalize poor women and men of color, thereby justifying their imprisonment and allowing the racist structures that affect access to employment, health care, education, and housing to go unrecognized.

Kum Kum Bhavani and Angela Davis[1]

Perhaps the most important thing I learned was about democracy, that democracy is not our government, our constitution, our legal structure. Too often they are the enemies of democracy. . . . What did I learn? That ordinary people are capable of extraordinary acts of courage. That those in power who confidently say "never" to the possibility of change may live to be embarrassed by these words.

Howard Zinn[2]

For those who seek justice and equality, democracy is a task. For those who seek dominance, democracy is theater. Democracy is dynamic and contentious. It is negotiated, subverted, unmasked, falsified, and used to coerce, by both powerful and ordinary people. It is won by people whenever repression is resisted. Joy James argues that the task of advocates for the socially excluded, is to expand "democratic practices by curtailing state abuses, particularly the racialized and sexualized manifestations of violence that victimize people of color, blacks, women and the poor."[3] James argues for a theory of social change that comes from ordinary peoples' struggles against state violence and for social justice. She rejects theories that are not embodied in those struggles, particularly those of academic theorists whose conversation "deradicalizes as it inbreeds, while the intellectual-interrogator takes precedence over the activist-intellectual."[4]

Democracy, for James, demands risk. "People who resist impoverishment and violence at times seem discouraged by elite academic discourse, the low threshold of political courage it inspires, as well as its truncated visions of radical change."[5] Patricia Hill Collins, too, is critical of intellectual theorists "who keep the language of resistance yet denude the theory of actual effectiveness [because] theory is given back to the people in a form that, because of the language used, becomes unusable for political struggle and virtually unrecognizable. The result is a discourse critical of hierarchical power relations that simultaneously fosters a politics of impotence."[6]

Radical change demands social transformation of unjust social structures and practices, but visions of change that will affect the lives of incarcerated mothers and their children need to have multiple strategic goals: structural changes (transformation practices) and policy changes (reforms) that will mitigate immediate social threats from state institutions (the criminal justice system, child welfare, social welfare, etc.). It is only because of the reform struggles of advocates and former prisoners separated from their children that any relief for families has been advanced. The picture book project, which allows mothers to read books to their young children by tape cassette; community/church groups who drive children to prisons two hours away; transition (from prison) houses that offer women wraparound support services to rebuild their lives and families—have all made a difference for families. Lawyers and activists from organizations like CLAIM (Chicago Legal Advocacy to Incarcerated Mothers) in Chicago have fought child welfare and prison personnel to keep families together rather than remove children to state care. An organization in Albuquerque, New Mexico, Peanut Butter and Jelly, created a holistic community-based advocacy program for incarcerated mothers and their children twenty years before the current explosion in the ranks of incarcerated mothers. In Seattle, Washington, Capacity for Justice (CFJ) addresses issues of health care for the families of the incarcerated. CFJ reveals the many influences that affect the health of these families, and CFJ has uncovered the fragmentation of services that overlooks or suppresses the relationships between social inequity and health problems.

These reforms have saved lives. Reforms, then, are recommended cautiously and specifically to stop immediate threats to imprisoned women and to the families of the incarcerated. What follows is a cautionary analysis of the ways in which reforms have been used to reestablish hierarchies of power and control, as well as examine the ways that women's advocates have won relief for incarcerated women through legal and social reforms.

LEGAL REFORM

Law has historically been used to legitimate race, class, and gender inequities. Yet feminist legal advocates' reform efforts, aimed at minimizing damage to incarcerated mothers and their families, indicate that the law is a site of struggle. "Thus the potential for using law to facilitate liberative struggle is real, but success is likely to be hard to come by—the struggle may fail or, worse, prove counterproductive over time."[7] But from time to time, legal and human rights advocates have won critical mitigations of threats to incarcerated women.

Nina Siegal has shown that throughout the 1990s legal and human rights groups have successfully litigated to stop physical and sexual abuse of women in prison.[8] In 1993, the National Women's Law Center filed a class action suit against the District of Columbia Department of Corrections for sexual misconduct and discrimination against women—and won. Lawyers in Georgia filed a complaint of sexual misconduct that included allegations of rape by prison guards. Although seventeen guards were indicted but none convicted, the prison at Milledgeville, Georgia, was closed and the women prisoners transferred. A sexual misconduct suit by three women prisoners in a federal facility in Pleasantville, California, against the Federal Bureau of Prisons was settled for $500,000 with stipulations for changes in women's treatment.[9] These interventions thwart brutality for some, while working for long-term structural change.

In 1996, a Human Rights Watch report (and before a 1990 Amnesty International report) exposed repeated sexual and human rights violations of women prisoners. Such exposés have effected critically needed reforms. Nevertheless, the lives of incarcerated mothers and their children remain hidden. Every reform has been wrenched from a system that considers these populations worthy of punishment but concede that excessive force or sexual misconduct must be checked if and when it is litigated or made public.

Laureen Snider notes,

> Legal action is sometimes important not because law in itself will increase the power of women, for history shows repeatedly that law has limited independence from structural forces, and limited potential to act as an independent instrument for social change. But legal battles may be a means to an end; the end being to increase the power of women on ideological, political and economic levels.[10]

Clearly, however, law's reform victories are most effective when targeting concrete rights to health care, low-income housing availability, child care, protections against termination of parental rights (except in cases of horrific abuse), living wages, Medicare, prisoner rights, and so forth.

REFORMS AS COVER-UPS

Reforms, like democracy, can be theater in which governing actors address publicly identified violations. The reforms function to lower scrutiny by convincing the public that human rights violations in prison are exceptional and fixable. Reforms (welfare, child welfare, and sentencing reform) are often the scaffold that symbolically masks state violence or social abandonment. Instead of offering remedy, the reforms reinforce the power of governing bodies to control and coerce stigmatized populations.

The failure of reforms has led many to argue for abolition of prisons. Karlene Faith illustrates the way in which governing bodies (in this case Canadian) co-opt liberating interventions and practices. In 1995, the long-ignored brutalization of female prisoners was exposed as a result of a Canadian video broadcast. The video showed a SWAT-like team of helmeted, masked, and booted male officers in a nighttime raid and strip search in which eight sleeping women in segregation cells were stripped naked, shackled in handcuffs and leg irons, and then subjected to body cavity searches. This action was retributory punishment "because they had been threatening to the guards in the days preceding the assault."[11]

As a result of this broadcast, the stalled 1990 recommendations of a Canadian prison-reform task force appointed by the solicitor general were incorporated into a government plan to open regional women-centered prisons and a healing lodge for First Nation women. "These were to be caring, empowering, supportive facilities in which punishment would no longer be the guiding principle. The task force was an example of participatory democracy in action. The inclusive process included hundreds—activists, feminists, First Nation women, women and human rights organizations."[12] The Canadian Correctional System agreed that the healing lodge would allow elders as counselors, healing circles, and the lodge, set amidst the beauty of Saskatchewan prairie and hills, would be without locks.

But the experiment was over when there were suicide and escape attempts. The regional institutions were changed from minimum-security to maximum-security prisons, equipped with hi-tech surveillance devices and razor-wire-topped fences; the number of prison guards was increased, and "women's cell spaces in Canada have nearly tripled since 1993."[13] There was no effort made to find out why women attempted to kill themselves or go on the run. Advocates concluded that in spite of "pastel walls and living units . . . the negative consequence of these new prisons has been to illustrate the impossibility of creating a community involving freedoms, responsibilities, and choices within a 'correctional' penological enterprise. . . . For real change to happen, prisons must be abolished, with investment instead going to schools, occupational training, decent employment, social services, and the rights of the most marginalized women [and men] in Canadian society."[14]

Not all reforms are so clearly compromised and politicized. What follows is an example of well-intentioned reforms that can extend and reinforce the surveillance net. Overall, the restorative justice model falls into the category of well-intentioned reforms that have been co-opted by the state but have also been successfully used to divert youth from incarceration.

RESTORATIVE JUSTICE OR TRANSFORMATIVE JUSTICE?

Howard Zehr directed the first restorative justice victim offender conferencing program in the United States. Initially the restorative justice model was employed in small, provisional circles in North America and New Zealand in the 1970s.[15] The restorative justice model was based on communal models of Native American, Canadian First Nation peoples, and Maori peoples in New Zealand for dealing with threats to both the community and individuals.

The purpose of the restorative justice model is to benefit the victim, the offender, and the community. The model addresses (a) the victim's injuries and needs, (b) the offender's accountability for rectifying harms they have caused, and (c) a collaborative process that involves all stakeholders: victim, offender, a mediator, and the community.[16] Often the process involves the offender's restitution to those harmed, and more broadly, services to the community. A 2002 restorative justice study of the responses of victims and offenders in five countries found that "the vast majority of participants find the experience satisfactory; fair and helpful . . . [and] offenders going through the conferencing approaches often have lower levels of re-offending than they did before compared with similar groups of offenders who did not go through the conferencing."[17]

The restorative justice model has been incorporated into the criminal justice system's presentencing diversion processes and in postsentencing parole applications. There are three models: (1) the victim offender mediation (VOM) model, (2) the family conferencing group, which involves family and friends of both the victim and offender, and (3) the circle group, which can also involve a broader family and community group. The form most often used by the state (VOM) is a highly structured procedure that insists on the neutrality of the mediator, and a proscribed preinterview with the victim and offender in which specific narratives related precisely to the harm caused and experienced are addressed. No counter or alternative narratives are encouraged.

The American Bar Association endorsed restorative justice in 1994, and the national Office of Juvenile Justice and Delinquency Prevention (OJJDP) has promoted the Balanced and Restorative Justice Project,[18] which solicits volunteer mediators to engage in a process that has diverted many young people from court adjudication to mediation centers in local communities. Occasionally, as in the Shakopee, Minnesota, Citizen, Victim's and Offender's Restoring Project (in 2000), the project takes place in a prison for women. The VOM model of restorative justice has won both popular support and official appropriation. And there's the rub.

Critics charge that appropriation by the state signals an expansion of surveillance into communities, and involves new but unofficial citizen legal "officers." The mediators, however determined to remain neutral, nevertheless hold the power position in the process. It is a process that espouses strict neutrality, but its norms remain culturally, politically, and economically part of the dominant judicial model and discourse.

Researchers Bruce Arrigo, Dragan Milovanovic, and Robert Schehr see the VOM procedure as linked to the retributive (punishment) discourse of the judicial process.[19] In this way they see the model as reproducing an alternative form, not of restorative justice, but retributive justice that is more benign but nevertheless maintains the status quo. They see limitations for offenders who are "healed" by acknowledging the harm they have caused, seeking restitution, and by accepting dominant cultural/institutional norms.[20] And the victim, too, is caught in a discourse process that tends to flatten out their pain. What follows is a critique by Arrigo, Milovanovic, and Schehr that incorporates their criticism of the effects on victims; the authors also cite Sara Cobb, who is concerned about violent harm to victims, particularly to women who have been raped.

> VOM removes [indeed, sanitizes] the presence of violence by replacing the rights-based discourse characteristic of adjudication processes with the needs-based discourse appropriate to relational cases. As Cobb suggests, this process delegitimizes the voice of the victim through a "domestication process." This phenomena refers to the act of perpetrating the oppression of women by refusing to acknowledge the actual violence perpetrated against them…the mediation process assumes a veil of moral neutrality in which anything may be said by anyone in the session and it [ostensibly] will not be judged as possessing any greater or lesser degree of legitimacy . . . through the assumption of a *laissez faire* morality, persons harmed are denied any meaningful acknowledgment of the pain they have experienced.[21]

The outcome of delegitimizing the victim's voice is not what proponents of the restorative model intend. Howard Zehr, for instance, insists that restorative justice must begin with victims whose needs are ignored by the criminal justice system and their very involvement in a judicial process can be a form of revictimization. "Victims often feel control has been taken from them by the offenses they've experienced—control over their properties, their bodies, their emotions, their dreams."[22]

Further, Zehr has responded to one of the most incisive critiques of restorative justice, which asks how victims and offenders can be justly restored to a system that is structurally unjust.[23] Zehr acknowledges that "there may be larger obligations beyond those of offenders: for example, the social injustices and other conditions that cause crime and create unsafe conditions."[24] Nevertheless, the fundamental problem with the restorative justice model, however well intentioned, is that it is not a true alternative to the retributive model. Restorative proponents' willingness, even eagerness, to have the model appropriated by a system based on retribution hardly suggests an alternative. Zehr states that most referrals will come from the criminal justice system—either from police officers, prosecutors, probation officers, judges, or even from prison officials. "Restorative justice approaches may also be used in conjunction with, or parallel to, prison sentences."[25] The social context and discourse within which restorative justice operates is still one of punishment, not civil wrongdoing.

In spite of these critiques, many legal advocates for youth insist that diverting a teenager from jail or prison trumps incarceration that is often life-destroying. While youth advocates recognize restorative justice's amplified surveillance dangers, its romanticized notion of community coherence and accountability, its cultural and political conformity norms, its inability to confront violence and trauma against victims, and finally, the narrow, individualistic terrain of its discourse and procedure, they still attempt to use the reform for purposes of diversion of youth from the soul-slamming experience of incarceration.

Restorative justice, like most reforms within the criminal justice system, fails to address the social inequities that override enforcement, judicial, and penal policies. At the macro level the growing practices of restorative justice diverges from a practice of transformative justice. Such a practice, disentangled from the criminal justice system, would involve community agents willing to promote racial/gender justice and political and economic critical literacy. These curriculums and transformative practices would promote social/economic justice and nonviolent solutions, as well as promote transitional support in the form of employment, housing, and health and child care.[26]

Ironically, most youth diversion programs utilizing the restorative justice model are directed at male youth. The social imperative to control irruptive male youth marks theses young men as more dangerous and more scrutinized. Although female incarceration has exploded, female youth have been incidentally part of restorative justice mediations. Perhaps gender stereotypes have benefited young women in this case. But if reforms ultimately forestall transformative justice, when it comes to mothers caught in the maw of incarceration, the question of using the least damaging reforms to mitigate its effects on families becomes critical. It is for this reason that this book ends with a resource listing a number of reforms—mother/child programs that exist within prisons, mother/child transition programs that are state sponsored, independent transition programs, and most importantly, legal/human rights advocacy and family advocacy organizations focused on transformative justice.

SOCIAL CHANGE AND GLOBALIZATION

Transformative justice demands policies that address the feminization of poverty, which has shaped the explosion in women's incarceration. This research has argued that no reform is sufficient to change the current increase in incarceration with special focus on mothers and the devastation of their families. A transformative strategy for change must address not only the racialized criminalization of women and the feminization of poverty (two processes that maintain social inequities in America), but such a strategy must also address globalization. Globalization has shaped both the expansion of the prison industrial complex and the extraction of social and economic capital from poor communities. Thus globalization has propelled the feminization of poverty.

Globalization, begun in the 1970s, is a process by which national economies and markets have become more consolidated and allowed a free, rapid transfer of specific cultural knowledge, goods, and capital, internationally. This process, which has privileged transnational corporations, has produced the greatest transfer of wealth, from the poorest nations to the richest, in the history of the world. For example, more than 100 countries have slid into economic decline and ruin since the 1970s; 4.4 billion people in the poorest nations live on $2 per day, 1.3 billion live on only $1 per day, and 840 million each day go hungry while, according to the United Nations, 15 of the richest people possess more wealth than the combined gross domestic product of all of sub-Saharan Africa.[27]

This transfer of wealth has been accomplished through: (a) a technological information revolution that has allowed corporations fiscal and productive mobility; (b) deindustrialization, which eliminated skilled and semiskilled workers and left massive social and economic dislocation; and (c) privatization and an elimination of social welfare, which has devastated poor communities, especially affecting the urban poor and farmers displaced by agribusiness. The loss of manufacturing jobs has left lower working-class neighborhoods fractured: beginning in the 1980s, more Americans are homeless than during the Depression; the number of families without health care has risen; urban schools have become battlegrounds; the drug wars have led to increased drug use; the "beloved community" has become more dream than reality; the primary capital flowing through many inner-city neighborhoods is drug money, prostitution money, and liquor sales; and the U.S. prison population has exploded. The blame for this deterioration has been laid on the moral failure of poor people, especially black and brown youth, immigrants, single mothers of color, and of course, drug users.

The socioeconomic pressures resulting from globalization's neoliberal economic policies have left poor countries in the global south desperate, and in the impoverished sectors of the north social exclusion has severed traditional communal networks resulting in an unraveling of the social protections of the poor. Both globalization and the racialized war on drugs account for women's increased incarceration and the woeful disregard of their children in the north. Their children, seen as appendages of the socially damaged, are cast into expendability. In summary, women's increased incarceration is related to three factors: (1) the effects of the breakdown of communal networks of care in poor communities, which results from (2) global policies that atomized working-class communities, and (3) Reagan's war on drugs.

Julia Sudbury argues that the neoliberal policies of the World Bank and the International Monetary Fund (the two international fiscal institutions that set structural adjustment lending policies for third world nations) have led to the "racialized feminization of poverty."[28]

> The concrete effects of the racialized feminization of poverty have been that women of color in the global north have been hit by cutbacks in welfare, shelter, day care and social programs. Because women carry the primary burden of feeding, clothing and caring for children and elderly relatives, they come under immense pressure when public services are cut back.[29]

Sudbury argues that the only effective way to keep mothers and children from the deleterious effects of incarceration is prison abolition. Abolition alone affects the profit-making capacity of the prison-industrial complex with its links to politicians' affiliation with corporate servicers and constructors of prisons and jails, its trend toward corporate privatized prisons, and the massive employment of carcel personnel.[30] Abolition demands a reimagination of justice and new solutions for transgressive acts. Nevertheless, abolition alone cannot address the inequities that produce social exclusion and racialized female impoverishment, but it can cut off further destruction of families and the warehousing of "expendable" populations.

In identifying the macro global and domestic policies that shape women's incarceration, there is no intention to suggest that social–economic structures overdetermine incarcerated women's fate. The testimonies in this book attest to women's resistance and agency in spite of structural obstacles. Increased imprisonment of women, situated in a global context of the increased wealth of the few and the increased poverty of the many, is also a result of racialized and gendered policies of the state. Neil Websdale and Meda Chesney-Lind consider "the imprisonment of women in general, and more specifically of those who have killed their abusers, as forms of state violence against women."[31]

CURTAILING STATE ABUSE AND EXPANDING DEMOCRATIC SPACE WHILE WORKING FOR ABOLITION AND SOCIAL TRANSFORMATION

Those advocates who work to curtail state abuses against incarcerated women and their children have opened up democratic space even when government and criminal justice doors slam against their efforts. The importance of shrewd concrete reform work is that it blunts abuse and neglect against suffering families. Chapter 11 examines remedies that can make postincarceration less stressful for families and former inmates. The implementation of policy changes have invariably resulted from arduous, lengthy legal battles, from the organizing efforts of community justice groups composed of former prisoners and their allies, from individuals working within the criminal justice system who see the futility of punitive policies that hurt families, and from the relentless campaigns of community and family justice groups—in summary, from ordinary people who demand change.

11

WHAT IS TO BE DONE IN THE MEANTIME?

In South Africa . . . the rights of children were deemed so important by the government that the legislature declared that all mothers of children under the age of twelve should be released from jail...There is also a new African charter on the rights of the child that allows minors to participate in the discussion of their economic and social rights.

Robert Drinan[1]

Community-based sentencing should be the norm for primary caregiver parents who are convicted of non-violent offenses.

Joanne Archibald[2]

Ultimately, alternatives (to incarceration) will be just only when we have removed biases from our mechanisms for apprehension, adjudication and sentencing. . . . To demand alternatives as the sentencing norm requires that we simultaneously express our underlying value that imprisonment became our last resort as a response to crime.

JusticeWorks Community[3]

Diana Delgado's spiral of trauma and dislocation began after her mother died when she was twelve years old and she was "thrown out in the streets."[4] A child herself, she learned early to live by her wits.

By sixteen years of age she was involved in an abusive relationship and bore a child who died of SIDS (Sudden Infant Death Syndrome). "These events played a major part in my drug use. I took drugs to medicate the pain."[5] Her first arrest was not for a crime she committed, but her willingness to protect her boyfriend. The second time, however, it was because she wrote bad checks. Her second incarceration was the beginning of her recovery because she was able to get into a treatment program. Currently, as the advocacy coordinator for Chicago Legal Advocacy for Incarcerated Mothers (CLAIM), Diana has become a powerful spokesperson before legislative committees, media and press, as well as community groups and the families of prisoners. She makes no one comfortable, however, by elevating her intelligence, her recovery, and her reunification with her four children. She is steely, almost clinical, in describing the damage to her children.

My incarceration was painful and traumatic for my children. I was in Lincoln Correctional Center, a four-hour drive from my home, which made it nearly impossible for my family [her grandparents took her children in] to bring my children to see me. It will take them years to heal from this separation. They felt abandoned and hurt, and their reaction was to rebel in school and at home. They have low self-esteem and feel like nothing matters. My daughter is the one who has been affected the most, for we were never able to bond like a mother and daughter should. She was born while I was in jail, and we were separated soon after her birth . . . her teacher has noticed her continuing need for unlimited attention. We need extensive long-term counseling. We can never reclaim that lost time.[6]

The lost time is a space that marks both mother and children with psychological wounds that they will carry into a future as bravely or terrified as their spirits can manage. This trauma is so invisible publicly, but to the parent and children it is the ghost that inhabits even their victories. Some children, like Joanetta's daughter Leona (the first family narrative in this book) bear public scars, in Leona's case, alopecia, where the child's hair falls out entirely. One of Diana's children also has alopecia. All of Diana's children's grades fell. "I have traumatized them in ways you can't imagine."[7]

But what about her own trauma as a child and later as an incarcerated mother? Diana considers herself lucky because she was one of ninety-eight women who were permitted to go into a drug rehab program. But Lincoln Correctional Center houses 1,000 inmates—what of the other 902? Although Illinois has desisted from the practice of shackling women in labor, Diana was shackled for the entire nineteen hours of labor with the daughter she is still trying to rescue. Currently, women are unshackled during labor, but handcuffed to their beds immediately before and immediately after delivery. They have forty-eight hours with their baby and then must give the infant to a relative or to the state. Although mothers may have given the name of a designated relative caretaker to a caseworker, if they deliver early or late and can't reach a relative within the designated time frame, they can lose the baby to state care.

An eleven-year-old nationwide survey of state prison wardens by J. D. Wooldredge and K. Masters indicates that only 48 percent had policies stipulating care for pregnant inmates.[8] Changes to these policies have invariably come from the organizing efforts of people like Diana. If a primary strategy is to stop locking up nonviolent offenders—thus obviating reforms that demand, minimally, prenatal care for pregnant inmates, drug rehab, a medical analysis of preexisting health care issues, nutrition and vitamin supplementation and well-baby parenting classes—a secondary strategy is community-based residential programs for pregnant inmates. What is needed are state-funded programs that offer substance abuse treatment; mental health care services; medical treatment and prenatal care with links to area hospitals for delivery; family relationship counseling; and comprehensive reentry and transition support that begins with entrance into the program and focuses on employment, reunification with children, high school completion opportunities, and access to college and vocational courses. Diana Delgado, along with advocacy groups like her organization CLAIM and the Chicago Coalition for the Homeless, fought for just such a community-based center—and won. The limitation, of course, is that the state-funded pilot residential program for pregnant inmates will serve only one hundred women.

CORRECTIONAL FACILITIES–NURSERIES/CHILDREN'S CENTERS

In addition to strategies for community-based residential centers for nonviolent offenders—especially those who are pregnant—there are correctional facilities nationally that have responded to the needs of mothers and children. One of the pioneer programs is New York's Bedford Hills Correctional Facility. Funded by New York's Department of Correctional Services, the program is administered by Brooklyn's Catholic Charities Office. They have a prison nursery that allows a mother to be with her baby for one year. Mothers involved in the program receive pre- and postnatal care, parenting classes, and a support team to help the mother decide, early on, who her child's caretaker will be, and discern a discharge plan that will support her reunification with her child and family. In addition to the mother's nurturing of her baby, volunteer *cuddlers* provide baby care and day care assistance while Mom is attending classes or completing work assignments. A Columbia law professor supervises law students who staff a weekly foster care and child custody clinic. Additionally, volunteers drive older children from Bronx and Brooklyn neighborhoods to the Bedford Hills Prison in order to spend a day or stay overnight, or for the children's summer program. The children stay with local host families and visit their mothers daily for two weeks while doing camp-type activities such as swimming and baseball. The Children's Center, where the children visit their mothers each morning, offers games, contests, a library, and a playhouse corner.[9]

Shakopee Women's Prison in Minnesota allows the child and mother to have weekend and vacation periods together, for which they are provided with homelike settings. Baltimore City's Health Department has a Healthy Start Program, which offers holistic services to pregnant women in the City Detention Center, and Johns Hopkins Center for Addiction and Pregnancy has designed a program to assist recovering addicted mothers to deliver healthier infants.[10]

The most successful parent-child programs are those that elicit collaboration and input from both the mothers and children. Prisoner committees that shape and decide the content and process of these programs are invariably more creative, effective, and prisoner endorsed.[11]

RE-ENTRY: PITFALLS AND POSSIBILITIES

The problem of reentry for the rising number of incarcerated mothers is a national crisis graver than the transition programs provided mostly for young men of color who are spit back unto the streets after serving time for felony convictions, with little hope of landing a job. The reentry process is more problematic for mothers, precisely because (1) they are economically responsible for children; (2) most enter prison without employment or a high school diploma; (3) they have often used up entitlement to welfare, which is cut off after five years; and (4) if the state has their children, they must participate, without fail, in several parenting, counseling, and drug testing programs, and show a permanent address and salaried work in order to regain their children, all of which, without transition programs, are difficult if not impossible to achieve.

In Cook County, Illinois, a survey found that 53 percent of the women entering Cook County Jail reported being homeless 30 days before their incarceration and 54 percent were not employed 30 days before going to jail. Over 80 percent of those reporting were mothers, and almost half (45 percent) of the women reported that they had been previously jailed two to five times![12] The revolving door of recidivism is predictable if poor, homeless, often sick, addicted, or mentally ill women cannot access programs or transition support services that can help them find housing, health care, work, drug rehab programs, and a way to negotiate the myriad paperwork demands required to access services from child welfare, mental health programs, welfare, and so forth.

Sister Kathy Nolan notes that there are 3,000 Illinois women incarcerated, all of whom will eventually need transition services, but there are less than a handful of community-based transition centers available—almost all of them with a sixteen-bed capacity. We know these programs are successful at lowering the recidivism rate. Grace House, where Kathy Nolan worked, for instance, began in 1994 as one of the first community-based transition centers in Illinois. The state recidivism rate for former women inmates is 65 percent. Grace House has a recidivism rate of 18 to 20 percent. Grace House begins with a needs assessment process, then offers women drug recovery and family reunification services. Sadly, according to Kathy, it is almost impossible for most to regain custody even if termination of parental rights has not yet occurred. Because women have only twelve months (at times mercifully extended to 18 to 22 months) to accomplish all the requirements demanded by the Department of Children and Family Services, it is often too late to catch up. Kathy did not see one woman gain custody of her child between 2001 and 2004. Moreover, in addition to the stigma of being an ex-offender, the women's lack of educational credentials makes job placement difficult. In the first seven years of her work at Grace House, Kathy Nolan never saw one woman able to pass the GED.[13] Even with a high school diploma or college degree (a rarity), many job sectors are not legally permitted to hire former felons. For example, child care, nursing, home health care, education, and security are prohibited employment sectors for former felons.

CLIMBING A MOUNTAIN OF OBSTACLES WITHOUT EVEN A WALKING STICK

The National Women's Prison Association and Home, Inc.[14] and the Chicago Coalition for the Homeless have documented the pile-up of obstacles confronting women exiting prisons or jails.

First, the 1996 welfare reform law only provides limited welfare support for those who work at jobs paying $8 an hour or less. In East

Harlem, the *new* welfare, Temporary Aid to Needy Families (TANF), is referred to as Torture and Abuse of Needy Families.[15] A number of states will not grant TANF benefits to people with drug felonies (80 percent of women convicts) or those with parole or probation violations.[16]

> Under the current system, someone who applies for welfare is lucky to get any benefits. More likely, the family will be diverted—sent to a food bank, told to apply for child support from an absentee parent, or assigned to a training program designed to keep them searching for a job. Those who make it through the process may see their benefits cut for any of a multitude of infractions (including, in some cases, having a child who regularly skips school).[17]

In Chicago, 29 percent of the women surveyed in Cook County Jail reported that within the year prior to their incarceration they had been cut off welfare or had an application denied.[18] How can a mother without a work history or a home previous to incarceration immediately find a job when she may lack a permanent address, has most likely *not* been in a drug rehab program in prison, and must negotiate reuniting with children who are troubled, angry, or withdrawn? Finally, if she finds work, how can she possibly afford day care, rent, and food on an $8-per-hour job?

Landlords can legally deny housing to former felons if they consider them a threat. Moreover, public housing authorities can deny housing to any felon for a lifetime. Some states, such as Illinois, have five-year bans on public housing availability to former drug felons. Each state housing authority has discretion in deciding the length of bans and exceptions to these prohibitions. These prohibitions have driven many families into shelters, which often results in the thwarting of the best intentions of former inmates. In Illinois, "women without housing are twice as likely to be detained more than six times."[19]

There have been few studies that analyze the health needs of incarcerated women. Many suffer from communicable diseases such as HIV, TB, and hepatitis. "Upon re-entry, treatment is inaccessible until a complex public assistance application process, which is dependent on a permanent address, is completed."[20]

Reunification with children is fraught with pain and requires enormous emotional insight and patience from mothers with fragile and guilt-ridden identities. They must be prepared to accept their children's rage or despair; they must be prepared to negotiate new "rules" with relatives to whom they owe a great deal and who may be carrying a good deal of stored-up resentment.

If they have not had contact visits with their children during their incarceration (which is true for 50 percent or more of the mothers), they may be subject to a termination of parental rights upon their release.

STRATEGY RECOMMENDATIONS FOR USE UNTIL PRISONS ARE ABOLISHED AND RACIALIZED STRUCTURAL INEQUITIES AFFECTING THE POOR AND MARGINALIZED, ESPECIALLY INCARCERATED MOTHERS AND THEIR CHILDREN, ARE TRANSFORMED

Women's reentry researcher Patricia O'Brien wants a diversion of funds from prison construction to the building and staffing of community-based transition programs.[21] Moreover, there needs to be trained discharge planners and employment counselors in prisons who can begin comprehensive discharge support services long before women are about to exit prison. Illinois, for example, currently offers women a two-week preparation for reentry. This superficial assistance is offered after a two- to four-year period of confinement in which few, if any, preparatory courses or educational opportunities are offered, outside the GED. Not all of this is the fault of prison caseworkers. The fact is that there are few community-based transition programs available, public housing is often denied and landlords may deny felons rental availability, many jobs are out of reach, mental health and child welfare services are fragmented with one agency not aware of the other agency's relationship with families in need, and there are few slots available in drug rehab programs.

The Women's Prison Association and Home Inc. believes that successful reentry plans must begin when a women enters a prison or jail. A comprehensive assessment of her needs and those of her family must address all dimensions: housing, health, education, and job skills or lack.[22]

Without these links from the inside of prisons to the outside, and/or links to community-based transition programs, women and their children can't traverse the long climb to stability and safety.

Funds diverted from the prison-industrial complex (one of the most profitable industries in the United States) could fund: mental health and good quality health care and substance abuse programs, both within prisons and in communities; educational, employment, and vocational services within prisons and in communities; day care; low-income housing available to women leaving prison; and assistance given to the many poor women whose homelessness can be a precipitating factor in her family's unraveling and her own incarceration.

Policy changes that will help prevent women's imprisonment, reduce recidivism, and prevent the destruction of families are:

A. Lift bans on welfare benefits.

B. Repeal draconian drug laws.

C. Eliminate termination of parental rights within a 12- to 22-month period unless there is indication of severe abuse, and decide the best interests of the child on a case-by-case basis rather than a policy that fits all.

D. Provide public housing and Section 8 availability to former inmates.

E. Rescind exclusions from job categories.

F. Provide quality day care that is publicly funded.

G. Fund community adult high schools for former inmates; make Pell grants available for those who cannot afford college.

H. Make parole supervision requirements take into account family demands in the case of mothers (or involved fathers).

I. Involve former inmates in the shaping of policies and decision making; hire them to provide leadership, practical advice and advocacy to women exiting prison and needing the understanding of others who have been through their experiences and who have successfully survived the traumas and obstacles the women face.

J. Involve children in decisions that will affect their lives.

K. Ensure that when a mother is arrested, a community advocate, who will transition the children and uphold their rights, accompanies the police officer.

L. Provide fiscal subsidies and support services to caretakers of children.

M. Encourage and provide affordable, consistent telephone access between incarcerated mothers and their children, as well as ongoing, proactive access to child welfare agencies making decisions about their children's welfare and care.

N. Eliminate sexual harassment of women prisoners and the presence of male guards in women's prisons.

O. Make postincarceration health and mental health care provision a legally enforceable mandate.

P. Locate mothers in community centers proximate to their children; make visiting facilities nonintimidating for children.

Q. Offer community-based post-release services that address the effects of trauma on children and offer wraparound, comprehensive services to families.

R. Provide children with support groups that allow them to discuss their worry about their incarcerated parent in a safe setting and that help them to cauterize the wounding shame they feel.

S. Coordinate child welfare and law enforcement policies.

T. Mandate legal changes in child welfare agencies' relationships with: incarcerated mothers, their children, and the children's caretakers. Train designated workers in implementation of new policies. Utilize workbooks like Lois Wright and Cynthia Seymour's *Working with Children and Families Separated by Incarceration: A Handbook for Child Welfare Agencies* (Washington, D.C.: Child Welfare League of America), 2000.

U. Make available to all incarcerated mothers and their children the publication *Children of Incarcerated Parents: A Bill of Rights*, San Francisco Partnership for Incarcerated Parents, 2000 (copies available from Friends Outside, 2540 Pacific Avenue, #8, Stockton, CA 95204, 209-938-0727).

THE COST EFFECTIVENESS OF POLICY AND LEGAL CHANGES

The least interesting argument for making these changes is cost-effectiveness. Although the logic of profit in a capitalist system trumps all other concerns, postmodern theorists would suggest that political economy is too fractured for such bottom-line logic. The argument suggests that multiple, complex, rapidly shifting and counter-manding interests so impact any site of influence that the singular logic of economic interest is an insufficient explanation. To some extent this theory explains the irrationality of continuing to create massive social dislocation, debt, punitive and military policies that squander the social capital of millions, and so forth. Marion Wright Edelman expresses the irrationality of the failure to address the squandering of human potential.

America cannot afford to waste resources by failing to prevent and curb the national human deficit, which cripples our children's welfare today and costs billions in later remedial and custodial dollars . . . the question is not whether we can afford to invest in every child, the question is, can we afford not to?[23]

Edelman, one of America's most outstanding child advocates, is not arguing for enlightened capitalism. She is unequivocal in confronting America's moral failure: "First World privilege and Third World deprivation and rage are struggling to co-exist not only in our nation's capital but all over an America that has the capacity but not the moral commitment and political will to protect its children."[24] If morality has failed American policy makers, Edelman seeks to point out not only the unreasonableness of writing off the vulnerable poor—she is trying to show the self-defeating nature of fiscal irresponsibility.

The following research suggests the ways in which states, federal jurisdictions, and taxpayers could save not only lives, but also money, if cost effectiveness recommendations were implemented.

- Arizona passed legislation that sent all nonviolent drug offenders into drug treatment instead of prison. The state saved $2.6 million the first year after the implementation.[25]
- "A 1997 RAND Drug Policy Research Center found that that treatment is not only far less expensive than imprisonment, it is also 15 times more successful in fighting drug abuse, reducing recidivism, and preparing participants for stable and productive lives in the community."[26]
- Each year New York spends $68,000 to house an inmate in the city jail and $32,000 to bed prisoners in upstate New York for one year. In contrast, outpatient drug treatment costs $2,700 to $4,500 per year and residential treatment costs $17,000 to $21,000 per year.[27]
- A study prepared for the New York City Council found that the cost of housing a woman at the Rose Singer Center on Riker's Island was $60,000 a year compared to $18,000 a year to house her in a drug treatment center.[28]
- It costs between $35,000 and $40,000 to incarcerate women in Illinois, the majority of who were incarcerated for nonviolent drug-related offenses. According to researchers Susan George and Robert LaLonde:

A third of the women admitted to state prison in Illinois in FY 2000 were admitted for property offenses, the most common property offense in that category was retail theft under $150 . . . Forty-four percent of women admitted . . . were for drug offenses . . . possession of trafficking, writing bad checks and using stolen credit cards. . . . There is not a lot of benefit to society—at least in the economic understanding of benefit—of locking up someone who walked out of a store with a shirt, even if they have done it more than once.[29]

KEEPING OUR EYES ON THE PRIZE

The recommendations in this chapter have come from advocate organizations that intend to prevent harm to incarcerated mothers and their families. They know that reforms are cast within a national theater of punishment that publicly stigmatizes, objectifies, and makes spectacle of these families while simultaneously making invisible their pain and terror. Most know that no sooner is a reform enacted than governing and bureaucratic bodies can use it to expand rather than reduce carcel networks. They know, too, that the herculean process of litigating, organizing, and demanding reforms is a complex, labyrinthian process that must confront bureaucratic intransigence, control, and the racialized politics of punishment. Finally, they know that the superficial but relentlessly produced discourse on drugs and violence has popular support. Reform efforts are therefore aimed at concrete changes in policies of punishment and in creating counter discourses that humanize rather than demonize incarcerated mothers and their children. Their purpose is to publicly link the disparate discourses of women's incarceration, violence against women, and the social abandonment of the children of incarcerated mothers.

Reform advocates must outsmart co-optive policy makers rather than be seduced by reforms that detract from the inequality, social exclusion, and violence against women that is produced daily. Until the theater of terror that plays with deadly permission is confronted, the growing incarceration of women will continue.

WHAT EFFECTIVE ADVOCACY LOOKS LIKE

Wenona Thompson is a pragmatic revolutionary. A former inmate and mother of two, Wenona fights for reforms while demanding strategies and practices of transformation that confront the social exclusion of large sectors of poor people of color. Her radical critique and example of unrelenting hope and determination inspire others. Wenona Thompson's life and unflinching truth telling is an example of Howard Zinn's notion that ordinary people are capable of extraordinary courage. Wenona's story follows in chapter 12.

12

BEATING THE ODDS

I hate not having control
When I think I'm living
something happens to show
I have no control.
Control, control,
control over my human soul.
I hate not having any control.

Wenona Thompson[1]

For many, if not most, children of color living in barrios, ghettos, and on reservations, lack of control over their lives is a script they receive at birth. Their subjugation is achieved through institutions that discourage their agency and by a surveillance network that targets their bodies for control. This surveillance is invisible to mainstream America, just as their neighborhoods and reservations are part of the publicly hidden but hyperscrutinized other America. Whole segments of the youth population live with fear and terror daily in these invisible American corridors. Wenona Thompson, the child of an incarcerated mother, was one of these children. Wenona's mother came from a violent and abusive family. Her mother became an addict and repeated the violence she knew. Wenona only remembers her mother going in and out of jail and the anger she felt at her mother for her abandonment. Between the ages of eleven and sixteen she became a master of the streets and a master of survival. Wenona navigated a life of abandonment, poverty, and violence with ingenuity, and even as a young child, she resisted her annihilation.

I used to help people carry bags from Jewel for quarters to help my Mama get money for her habit. My friends made fun of me. I got angry. I became harder, impatient, ultimately violent. I stole, robbed, beat up those who disagreed. I'd smash up abandoned cars. I was so angry.

I didn't want to, but I hurt other people. It was part of the game to get what I needed. I remember thinking clearly how my life would end. There were three ways: I kill somebody, somebody kills me, or I would commit suicide. The reason I felt this way is that I began to see how people ignored me. When I was on the streets I kept saying to God, "Where you at?" Somebody said, "Why you don't go to church?" I thought, why would I go to church when I was born into this? I didn't choose to be.[2]

Eleven-year-old Wenona's anger at being ignored led her to resist invisibility. She took action, entering the game of the streets, to get what she needed. She recognized the danger, calculated the odds, and then navigated the projected violent outcomes. These choices are what she was given as a child. Her ingenuity belies the stereotypes that see the children of incarcerated mothers as passive victims who lack agency. Her rage is directed at exclusion and abandonment. Imagine a childhood in which each day demands tactics needed to survive in a war. Removing mothers from their children for nonviolent crimes leaves these children unprotected emotionally, physically and economically, even if the mother is dysfunctional, as was Wenona's mother.

The everyday lives of these children are rarely the subject of study, yet an examination of their daily survival strategies, negotiations with caretakers, teachers, child welfare workers, and other authorities, as well as the reconfiguring of their familial role when their mother leaves, reveals children's creativity and agency. In addition, an examination of their daily lives uncovers how they play the game of the streets, which is often the key to both their survival and endangerment. The context of Wenona's description of her youthful life on the streets is always her mother's incarceration, which she identifies as the precipitating event that plunged her family deeper into crisis.

The following is a poem Wenona wrote about the impact of her mother's incarcerations when she was eleven. She wrote the poem when she was seventeen.

The Day My Mother Was Sent Away

The day my mother was arrested was the beginning of my destruction.
No one will ever actually understand me until their mother
    is legally separated from them.
I know what my mother did was wrong or against the law, but I
    already don't have a father, now they done took away my mother.
I can't seem to understand this, for where is my mandatory love,
    attention, discipline, understanding and home education gonna
    come from?
A lot of people assume that my mother is the cause of these
    changes. But regardless of who causes such problems,
    the consequences are not solving them.
For so long I tried to make sense out of these state rules and regulations.
But for some reason I can't understand why there isn't an alternative
    punishment for crime-convicted mothers with babies.
I know this may not be true but are the state trying to rectify the
    problem, prolong it, or maybe just create something totally new?
Hmm, I truly don't know.
I'm now older with children of my own, facing many issues
    not only within myself, but also the issues of my mother, who
    I impatiently awaits to remeet
I sometimes ask myself if this punishment my mother and I are
    receiving is accurate. In all honesty, I say it is not, for this was my
    mother's first offense and the crime was not violent.
But still the state changed my goals and also the goals of my mother,
    my children, and my sister's and my brothers.[3]

This is a subversive poem, but not because it poignantly describes the effect on a child of the loss of her mother. Childhood grief at abandonment is not a surprise, but children's resistance is. What the poem subverts is mainstream adult policy assumptions about the passivity of these children. Wenona interrogates a culture that consigns her to the margins. Social critic bell hooks has said the marginalized react with despair or resistance. Wenona claims the margin as a place of agency, a place to refuse the authority of a system that has written her off.

Wenona has linked her youthful rage and terror, not to the pathological dominant interpretation, but to the loss of her own history. The devastating result of her mother's addiction was that her mother became mute about the past. Her mother offered no narrative to contest or explain her own or her family's pain.

I remember *wanting* to go to jail or DCFS because of my mother's drugs. She was very violent because of what she endured. But it was never talked about because she hasn't even processed it yet. We, as a people, are used to telling our stories orally, but when someone is strung out on drugs and they are carrying that history inside, then who is telling a true history? How could we respect that history if the person is strung out?[4]

Wenona's own resistance began with her refusal to hide and her determination to tell the truth, not only of her own life, but that of her people. Joy James notes, "Families and states often discourage storytelling that reveals their vulnerable proximity to, as well as culpability in, violence . . . telling the truth about family violence is viewed as destabilizing the family just as vocalizing state violence and human-rights abuses is portrayed as destabilizing the state."[5]

It is this silence about terror, with its disconnection from a source, which obliterated her mother's agency. Her mother's addiction resulted in the isolation and erasure of a self that was violated as a child. The beginning of healing for torture victims is the willingness to bring to speech the violence suffered. The fractured self becomes whole in breaking the stranglehold of silence that terror produces. Wenona's mother could not, would not, speak.

So that's why I was bound by design to repeat my mother's mistakes. [Somehow] I refused because my mother's life would make me voiceless. I refused the oppression of a system that says I can have no voice. It's pacification, like slavery. The elites pacify us, give us a little something to keep us quiet. We're still enslaved mentally by a system that's not seen [but] that orients others to do the job. We have education systems that improperly educate people to not know their purpose in life—some are trained to work from their neck down rather than their head [laborers]. Some don't even get that because single parents don't have the people around them or the resources to have job opportunities. They may as well be left for dead. We have hospitals that medicate and maintain social control. We have mental institutions that therapize and medicate people with toxic drugs that are more dangerous than the illness the person is facing.[6]

INCARCERATION

Wenona had been selling drugs for only two weeks when she was arrested. Her male partner was selling too, but he was sentenced to only thirty days. Though a teen, Wenona was transferred to adult court and got four years but served two and a half. Like so many youths who survive by their grit and willingness to fight to survive, Wenona presented as a tough, sassy teen. But she was naive about the law, about incarceration. She wanted to be locked up if it meant she'd get help. She was in pain and spiraling downward. More than anything her impulse was to find someone to listen, someone to know her story. Unlike her mother, Wenona understood that voice and story, however painful, was the beginning of claiming a self and wholeness.

When I got to jail I thought I'd be rehabilitated. [But] I ended up close to those who hated me and far from those who loved me. I waited and waited for someone to come and talk to me. Somebody to say, "Why did you want to throw your life away?" Nobody ever came. Nobody.[7]

It is not the isolation of incarceration alone that destroys. It is the message of disposability that such silencing produces. The feeling that Wenona had as a child—that she was ignored and that she didn't matter to people—was reproduced institutionally. These young people's stories are not heard because they don't count, and because they tell dangerous narratives. "Like the family, the state 'protects' itself from exposure and confrontation by discrediting or muting stories . . . stories that condemn sexual and racial violence are probably perceived as most disturbing, for they contest claims to moral legitimacy by the state."[8]

Alone, without an adult who listens, these young people do what they have always done on the streets. They listen to each other and cobble together dreams, jokes, and tears, to assure each other they understand what the world around them has ignored.

One day in my cell I wanted to die. But I decided if everyone gave up on me, I wouldn't give up on myself. I was confused . . . I didn't know the law and didn't understand the severity of my charges. My mother couldn't protect me. She had no words and she couldn't represent or advocate for me. I became my own guardian.

I wanted school. I began to write poetry. I was like a youth counselor to other girls. We talked at night about how our mothers were on drugs. A couple of times I woke up in the morning and to my surprise I found two different letters from girls telling their stories of abuse.[9]

REENTRY

When you come out your spirit is broken . . . sometimes guilt and shame keeps you from even trying for a job.[10]

**Wenona speaking at a Beyond Media Women
in Prison Panel**

Wenona describes two outcomes of incarceration: incapacitating shame and fear. These outcomes are predictable, reproduced yearly, and in the case of women, they are multiplying. How could these outcomes be understood in any possible way, other than as being intentional? That is, they are outcomes the state expects, allows, and continues to promote. Girls who use or sell drugs are out of control and the state's task is to reorder them to their gender role and their racial and structural place of invisibility. The social exclusion and racialized surveillance that Wenona experienced as a child was reinscribed on her body when she left prison. Every institution to which she turned re-marked her as stigmatized. When Wenona was released from prison she was homeless. When she applied to the Chicago Housing Authority for public housing she was refused because she was a felon.

When I was getting out, they didn't say, "Okay, you've been locked up for two and a half years we know you'll need help. We'll give you contacts in your community to get proper support for issues that you need." There was no advice or money to cover me until I found a job. When I got out at 17 and a half years old, I didn't even know how to use the transportation system because it had changed. All they gave me when I left was fear that if I did anything wrong, even though I needed to live, I would face the same walls again.[11]

Fear is what the state offers. "The emphasis on personal responsibility creates an atmosphere of public surveillance and minimizes public responsibility for change and redistributive social policy."[12] Wenona knows she is *watched*—watched because she is an ex-felon, watched because she is African American, because she is a mother, because her brother is an ex-felon, because her twelve-year-old nephew is in a juvenile facility. Surveillance, which happens to the privileged when they have to wait in airports and endure lengthy, intrusive searches, is daily and endless for those who are marked by exclusion, inequality, racism, regulation, and incarceration. The surveillance networks need not use violence to enact control. Fear, shame, and a sense of unending bureaucratic/institutional discipline can beat down the spirit of even sassy and smart young people. Wenona was sassy and smart, but she had to reclaim that spirit and her very sense of identity after imprisonment. She had changed. She had been lucky enough to go through drug rehabilitation in prison. She was no longer willing to hurt herself or blame herself for all that she endured as a child.

When I was released, I was a stranger. I'd changed but felt back in the same situation except that I wanted to avoid mistakes but had to live the same way.[13]

This situation constitutes the other America, where policies of exclusion hold down agency; where resistance or irruptive violence triggers spectacles of police roundups, rough-ups, and arrests intended as both symbolic and concrete lessons of control and subjugation. These spectacles deflect attention away from social injustice through performative rituals that criminalize individuals. Wenona must somehow live in these targeted neighborhoods and negotiate the chaos and violence that results from policies of social expendability. Moreover, she must protect her children from these terrors. And she must do it alone. She can't rely on her family because they have been caught in the maw of surveillance and punishment. She has tried to intervene with her sister who is on drugs. Mostly Wenona wants to keep her sister's three children from experiencing what she went through. But she is clear on boundaries. Her twelve-year-old nephew has already begun his time in the carcel network that especially surrounds black male children.

My sister's son doesn't show her respect. I know the reason. First of all, he has no true sense of who he is and who his father is and what is his family makeup. He doesn't respect his mother because she does drugs and is never there. So when my nephew came to live with me, I disciplined him. When I laid down the law my sister and nephew were surprised. I told him, "If you don't take it like this, they ain't never going to give it with love. They'll just shove it down your throat and you'll have to accept it anyway. It's best to come from me because I'm goin' to tell you the true nitty-gritty and I'm not goin' to take nothin' from you." He is in juvenile detention right now.

My sister has three kids and she's still on drugs. It hurts me to see how my little niece is. It's hard to see her grow up and know that she's facing so much. I was so mad at my sister I punched her. She takes so much of my energy that I need to do the work. [Wenona works as the director of Girl-Talk, a support program for female teens incarcerated in the Cook County Juvenile Detention Center.] My sister doesn't understand that I need support, too. I'm a little like Harriet

Tubman sometimes. I actually punched her because if she can't help me to help others, then get out of my way.

My sister's house has no heat. My ten-year-old niece is there with no food, no heat, nothin' to keep her a child. When I see that I think what can I do. So I take her out to dinner, tell her jokes. Then I look back at her mother and I see myself.[14]

Most of Wenona's family members look to her as someone who has made it. She graduated from college and has a job. Wenona's success is not simply her unswerving determination to help other youth avoid the traps and pitfalls laid for them by a system that teaches them to devalue, and blame themselves for social neglect and punishment. Wenona's task is to awaken in them their own truth. She wants the rage and sorrow they have turned on themselves and others to have true aim. She helps them understand their lives from a perspective of resilience. The majority of the female youth she works with in the Cook County Juvenile Detention Center have been physically or sexually abused.

The cultural discourse that has surrounded these young women during childhood has prepared them for jail or disposability. Their incarcerative task is to reflect on their bad choices. Wenona helps them remember another history: the frightened, abused children they were who possessed resourcefulness, grit and resistance that both hurt and saved them. Wenona and the young women in the Cook County Juvenile Detention Center are deconstructing a racialized cultural narrative about incarcerated females.

If we have a Constitution to protect freedom of speech and we don't share the truth of what these young people are going through, then America is not free. How many are aware of the [real cause] of their problems? So many grow to feel there's nothin' they can do. Why? Fear. When you have a young person who grows up in negativity and with problems and they grow to demonstrate that negativity, they're not looked at as somebody who was abused at an early age but they're told they're stupid, violent, crazy. There are institutions designed for them. No one is questioning the extended systems of oppression and inequality. No one is questioning this because there's a lot that takes our minds off this, designed to take our minds off this because there's a certain world order that a lot of people are not aware of. [Young people] are not educated about this; they don't have time to learn it; and some would be totally overwhelmed. So we have a lot of young people are feelin' like they made crucial mistakes even though they have come from poverty, violence, drugs, and poor educational systems. They feel they are not good enough.[15]

Wenona wants young women to fight a system that has destined them for control and destruction, all the while insisting that failure is their fault. Their social success, according to the metadiscourse they've received, will be achieved when they accomplish their gender roles as married, employed, sober mothers—in summary, when they adjust to white middle-class maternity standards. Wenona wants their rage and their refusal to serve as a counterdiscourse. She wants the young women to "outfox the fox," to *use* treatment programs to get free, not to get adjusted. She searches to find them community-based transition centers that are advocacy and asset oriented, and she encourages them to make choices that resist subjugation to assigned gender or racial roles, and to see themselves as young women who have rights. Wenona listens in order to allow space for the young women's stories. Together they are creating a new narrative that subverts the story of their failure. It is provisional, fragile discourse that is the beginning of the voices of their history.

INTERVENTIONS—GENDER-SPECIFIC INITIATIVES FOR AVOIDING FUTURE INCARCERATION OF WOMEN

In the years since Wenona's incarceration, the delinquency cases of females under age sixteen increased 89 percent between 1988 and 1997.[16] The increased incarceration of young women has also produced some remedies not available eleven years ago when Wenona was convicted. Research studies of confined female juveniles reveal that childhood experiences of abuse and neglect lead to risky, illegal acts and subsequent involvement with the criminal justice system. A 1998 National Council on Crime and Delinquency (NCCD) study shows a correlation between physical and sexual abuse of female youth and substance abuse. "According to their case files 95 percent of the girls [interviewed] were assessed as lacking a stable home environment."[17] The linking of the future incarceration of women to childhood experiences of violence and instability has been a significant breakthrough that has led to more gender-specific interventions in both community-based programs and correctional programs.

Programs that divert girls from incarceration are crucial. Although these programs address gender inequity, they rarely target social inequity, which is normalized in discourse about stable and unstable homes. Why, for instance, are 95 percent of these girls' homes considered unstable, and why are their impoverished neighborhoods and schools considered unstable? Such discourse does not address the social and economic stressors that led to their parent's incarceration or their family's dysfunctionality. The NCCD study revealed the generational repetition of outcomes of over half of the females interviewed—54 percent of the girls reported that their mothers had been arrested or incarcerated.[18] Although the NCCD study did not target the macro levels of social abuse and neglect that shape generations of poor women and children of color, the study did show the multiple forms of harm that lead to the future incarceration of girls.

The NCCD study did address racial inequity. It found that nationally, two-thirds of girls in the juvenile system are African American or Latino. Moreover, the study revealed racialized sentencing. "Although whites reported the most drug use, compared to other racial groups, they were significantly more likely to also report that their most recent charge was a probation violation."[19] The NCCD study recommends, at a minimum, more culturally appropriate interventions and services. Most significantly, this major study revealed the dismal level of programs addressing the needs of this population, particularly programs that can address the trauma these young women experienced. In fact, a psychiatric research study found that almost half of incarcerated girls have posttraumatic stress disorder.[20]

Beginning in the 1990s, PACE Center for Girls produced a culturally and gender-sensitive curriculum that addresses the multisystem paths that lead young women into involvement with the criminal justice system. PACE's curriculum—SMARTGIRLS!—was one of the first to offer an asset approach to being young and female rather than a deficit model. These curriculums, as well as others, have been used in community-based programs, and they've been used in incarceration facilities. Baltimore Maryland's Female Intervention Team (FIT) is a community-based program that assigns caseworkers to girls at risk for future incarceration and offers personal support, connections in their communities, and programs of support: academic tutors/computer courses, teen parenting groups, a Girl Scout program, and a rite-of-passage ritual and cultural celebration of entering womanhood. Two years after this program began, there was a 50 percent reduction in the number of girls sent to Maryland's secure facility; the following year there was a 95 percent decrease. FIT has not transformed the social conditions that continue to provoke girls to run away, end up on the streets after they drop out of school, break curfew, be drawn into prostitution, and experience abuse, rape, and sometimes drugs. But when the girls came in contact with the juvenile justice system, FIT provided a gender-sensitive and culturally supportive alternative to locking them up.

NORA: VIOLENCE, TRAUMA, AND A NEW PATH

Without community-based alternatives to lockup, the only chance for a young mother like Nora Acosta is a postprison transition program that offers drug rehabilitation and allows the mother to live with her child in a community setting with other mothers and children. La Entrada de Amistad in Las Lunas, New Mexico, is one such program. The mothers, who are all on parole, chose to live together and support each other and their children while receiving support services in a residential setting for six months.

Nora Acosta has black eyes and her dark hair falls over her shoulders. Her daughter Jasmine, who is seven, has the same wistful eyes and the same moon face as her mother. They are beautiful and quiet. Nora's delicate looks fit the stereotype of *lady*, until she tells her story. Then the other stereotypes sneak in—the ones that have branded Nora as painfully and irrevocably as a rancher might sizzle his brand onto the hide of cattle. Nora believed the branding—that she was a whore, an unredeemable crackhead, and a vile mother.

Nora Acosta was one of the first women to volunteer for the La Entrada de Amistad program, which opened in 2002. Nora, who is twenty-four, is seven or eight years removed from her wild youth, but she still fears parole on her own. As a youth her criminalization began because of parole violations. In fact, criminalization for many young women begins with parole violations—breaking liquor laws, breaking curfew, truancy, and so forth. Invariably, however, the young women's misdemeanors began when they ran away from abuse and ended up on the streets where survival led them to selling drugs or sex. The path to criminalization begins with their bodies or their mother's bodies, which receive the first wounds. As a child, Nora watched her father beat her mother. "My mom was all bloody all the time. I got in between his beating but then after that the beatings just became normal."[21]

Nora's father was a heroin addict who was killed in an accident when she was eight. But the trauma of her mother's abuse didn't leave her.

At twelve I experimented with sniffing spray paint. I grew up in a war zone in Albuquerque. I hung with gang members. We would steal stuff and sell it in Mexico. At thirteen, I met Jasmine's dad and I ran away to be with him. He was emotionally abusive, but I was so in love. He controlled me. Sometimes he'd say I was a "fat bitch" to humiliate me; then if I looked pretty he'd say I was giving too much to his male friends. He accused me of going out on him, but I would never do that because I loved him so much.[22]

At fourteen Nora was sent to a girl's school, which was a boot camp, because she violated her probation by breaking into a school. When she was fifteen she was pregnant with Jasmine. Her boyfriend worked at Burger King. She was selling drugs to make money, but she was not using crack until her boyfriend introduced her to smoking. She was arrested again four years later.

Before my eighteenth birthday, I was arrested. I went to New Mexico Girl's School. I was pregnant but still had to keep up the [rigorous] exercise routine. I told them I wasn't feeling well, but they didn't believe me and I went into labor and had an emergency c-section. The baby, Angelique, was two pounds. They took me to see her in the hospital every day. But they wouldn't parole me.

When I was released [I thought I'd be ready to take my baby home] but my boyfriend was drunk and he hit me. The cops took him to jail. I broke up with him. I thought my world had ended. I didn't show up at the hospital to see the baby. I signed over my rights to my baby to my aunt and uncle and I left my little Jasmine with my mother. I went to the streets. After two months I had to prostitute myself. I was a crackhead, alcoholic, heroin addict. I don't know how I survived walking the streets and picking up tricks. I didn't care about anybody.... A dope dealer who robbed me hit me with a shotgun.

I'm only twenty-four, but I feel like fifty.[23]

Nora wants more than survival now. She wants to turn her life around for her daughter, Jasmine. Nora believes her mother hung on, in spite of her father's abuse, for her sake and her brother's. She considers herself lucky that her mother took her daughter in and was willing to let her return to Nora, a mother Jasmine had not lived with. Both grandmother and daughter waited for Jasmine's choice. Each of these generations of females who've suffered have made choices that demanded bravery, generosity, and trust.

My daughter still trusts me. It's a miracle—when I went to prison my mom said she'd close the door on me if I didn't get it together. I'm just glad my mom didn't disown me. I'm lucky to have such a mother.

The transition with my daughter is tough. I'm learning to let her make her own decisions. She hasn't asked me why I abandoned her. Someday she will.[24]

Nora doesn't fully know yet why she abandoned her daughter, but La Entrada de Amistad has helped her critique the poisonous, self-hating messages that she absorbed. She refuses the stigma that brands her and women like her—*pintos*—which means tainted. Nora knows that she has chosen to live, and that the director of the program, who is a recovering addict, seeks to accompany her and her companions on their journey to wholeness. La Entrada de Amistad, which is a thirty-minute ride from Albuquerque, is not like the other programs available when women leave prison.

Here in New Mexico we don't have shit. They send you back to programs in war zones. There's Bridge—I left after two weeks. There was no process, no digging deep. WINNERS is just paying rent. They lock up the refrigerator to save money. There's no programs for women and children. Here, you are treated like human beings and they are generous. We get to have our children with us.

The only way you get through things is to open up the wound and clean it out.[25]

PEANUT BUTTER AND JELLY

La Entrada de Amistad is the brainchild of Peanut Butter and Jelly (PB&J Services), a program begun by Angie Vachio thirty years ago. What began in Albuquerque's south valley, with Angie's making peanut butter and jelly sandwiches for troubled children and offering services to preserve their fragile families, has grown to serve thousands of New Mexican families. PB&J offers an array of services to children and families who have experienced incarceration. One of its initiatives, ImPACT, offers a program to inmate parents beginning in the last year of their incarceration, which is designed to support parents in reuniting with their children. ImPACT offers workshops in parenting skills and in reunification with children, and caseworkers arrange visitation with children in a child-friendly atmosphere within the prison. Finally, ImPACT staff members provide follow-up support and services after release.

Some of the services PB&J offers following release are intensive home-based services for families that are isolated because of distance, or for a first-time mother who is isolated or unable to have family and mentors to support her parenting and bonding efforts. There are two PB&J therapeutic preschools for children from birth to five years of age. The Albuquerque preschool serves almost 300 toddlers, and the Bernanillo school serves 133. Each child's parent also attends two-hour classes four days per week. Attached to the schools are health service centers, which offer outreach nursing services in the Bernanillo area, particularly to outlying, rural areas. Additionally, PB&J provides ten vans to transport kids to school, on field trips, and to visit parents in prison.

PB&J is unique in philosophy and practice. It identifies the family's strengths and collaborate with the family in determining how they can meet their needs. It develops all programmatic responses to the children of incarcerated parents with the assumption that the child has experienced trauma. Thus its preschool is therapeutic. It recognizes that many parents also carry with them the effects of trauma.

"These kids have been through more than anyone can imagine," Angie Vachio says. "Until we take money from prisons and put it into treatment, nothing will change. Here in New Mexico we don't have decent treatment services. We need mental health services, we need a medical system for women, we need services that deal with trauma, and we need reintegration that effectively links parents back to their families. The recidivism rate in New Mexico is 80 percent. Here at PB&J it's 6 percent."[26]

There are other programs like PB&J that offer services to mothers and services that specifically target the trauma their children carry. In *The Children of Incarcerated Parents*, one of the authors, Denise Johnston, has a chapter titled "Interventions," which offers a descriptive listing of model programs that offer comprehensive services to parents, as well as interventions (preventative and therapeutic) that address separation and trauma reactions in children.[27]

In addition, there are community-based transitional residential centers, such as Providence House in New York, that offer families support but do not offer wraparound or therapeutic services for traumatized children. To some extent the participants create their own communal networks of support in these residencies. Providence House has six community-based transitional residences for women and children, especially mothers leaving prison who have no housing. Providence House has permanent housing that accommodates 150 women and children, mostly in Brooklyn, and they have transitional apartments where women and children live communally and where on-site staff offer services that link participants to community services and offer assistance with relocation and employment searches. A child care center provides day care and after-school care for children.

THE TRAUMA THEY CARRY

Tim O'Brien wrote a novel about his experiences in Vietnam in which he described the packs that soldiers carried mile after mile each day. O'Brien listed the weapons, radio equipment, transformers, shovels, ammunition, scopes, and other items the men humped into jungle thicket, across rivers, rice paddies, and over bomb-cratered, desolate fields. But the crushing weight that O'Brien was after was not back-breaking packs. O'Brien's narratives revealed the terror and trauma that was not visible. Soldier after soldier carried their packs, as tough, resilient trudgers. They couldn't or wouldn't talk about the horror of what they'd seen or done or feared.

Trauma silences. The silence is a prison. The children of incarcerated parents are twice traumatized. First, they are traumatized by the violence they have seen or by the terror of seeing their parent arrested and not knowing what will happen to their mother or themselves in that wrenching moment. Then they are traumatized by the shame and stigma that marks them and their mother as trash. These children do time long after their parent's incarceration. Without services that address trauma, these children will carry hidden, virulent anguish and humiliation that can lead them to self-destructive or socially destructive behaviors. Addiction is often the only way they can deal with their suffering. Like Vietnam vets, they carry survivor's guilt—trauma and shame that they couldn't prevent violence against a parent.

These children have been through wars. Not just President Reagan's drug wars, which were racialized wars against the poor, but also as a result of a globalized economy's privatization of social services and the elimination of social benefits that have left many on America's killing floors. The children of these wars attend schools and live in neighborhoods that are under siege. Social exclusion produces rage or despair or resistance. Too often the rage or despair is turned against those closest to them. Over and over research indicates that women incarcerated for nonviolent, drug-related crimes came from homes of abuse and violence.

THE FIDELITY OF CHILDREN

Martha Aragon is one of those mothers who was traumatized as a child by watching the abuse of her mother. Martha, like Nora Acosta, is one of the pioneer women at the Entrada de Amistad transition program in Las Lunas, New Mexico. When I visited Entrada de Amistad, Martha and her son, Patrick, sat off to the side observing when the other mothers and children were interacting. They clung to each other and seemed in their own world. Patrick has long dark lashes and a handsome face. He will soon be a young man but now, at twelve years old, he seemed only to want to stay at his mother's side. There was an aura of exquisite sadness about Martha. She was confounded by the mystery of her son's love in spite of what she'd put him through. She was determined to be successful in the program in order to regain custody of both her sons. Martha gave up on herself years ago but her sons, remarkably, have not: "My sons are the source of saving my life. I haven't been able to do it [recover from addiction] for myself.[28]

One wonders what the outcome might have been if Martha had a way to break the silence about the suffering of her mother who bore fifteen children fathered by an alcoholic who beat her relentlessly. Martha's sheepherder father beat her mother during pregnancy causing her to lose three children. Her baby brother died from pneumonia because her father wouldn't let her mother get help.

[Watching the abuse] cost me. I became a really angry person. Sometimes my mother hid us under beds or covered us with mattresses because my father had guns. [My mother] was the toughest person I knew, but she suffered so much. She's dead now but my father, who is 89, is still a whore. He took me in his truck when he went whoring.[29]

Martha's unraveling happened when she fell in love with David, "a wonderful man," and they moved to Alamagordo, New Mexico. He was killed in an auto accident and on the day she buried him, she went to visit her mother in the hospital. Her mother died the same day.

My mom was my best friend who was there for me and so was David. After that I went downhill. I started drinking, doing crack. I met a trucker, Carl, who was the father of my oldest son. We drank and fought. I went to jail for ninety days on an assault charge because I pulled a gun on him. Then I got a divorce.[30]

Martha picked up two more DUIs (driving under the influence). She spent six months in jail for the second charge. Her sister took her nine-year-old son in. When she received her fourth DUI, she got eighteen months and child welfare took her younger son, Patrick, and gave him to her aunt. "My sons went into trauma—kids truly suffer."[31]

When Martha received her fifth DUI and was given twenty-two months, she finally got into a rehab program, but her great aunt had died and the state put her son in foster care.

He's so traumatized. He says, "Ma, why did you leave me, why did you do this to me? Why can't I see my brother?" If I don't change my life, he'll become an alco-holic/addict because that's what happened to me because of the rage I felt at my father. I will do this program in order to get my boys back. I don't want them hurt again.[32]

Martha is pained by her son's questions, but she is facing them and facing herself. The rage Martha felt toward her violent father through-out her life was mostly directed at herself. She is a remarkably quiet and gentle person, and that sweetness may explain her son's fidelity in spite of her betrayal of their trust. Martha had understood herself as *pintos* and she was slowly killing herself until beginning rehab allowed her to believe a new narrative, one in which she had choices and two young people who loved her were waiting for her.

Martha's boys will have to do their own work to break the strangle-hold of shame and anguish at their separation from their mother. But they have an ally now who, with them, is writing a new history—one in which women have voices and boys can tell a new story about them-selves. It is a story about family members who clung to each other and forgave each other in spite of everything that happened. It's not a pretty or romantic or middle-class Anglo story because that would be a lie. It is a story about fear and anger and bravery—most of all it's a story about the power of children's love. And it is the story of their mother's decision to live. That decision was/is not her only act of resistance to the violence that pummels her life, but it is the most effective one.

MORE SOLDIERS OR AN END TO THE WAR?

There are many advocates for incarcerated mothers and their children who, like Tim O'Brien's pack-burdened foot soldiers, trudge on through jungles of legal and policy obstacles. They soldier on, exhausted from tending the fallen and fighting an elusive enemy, yet they consider resistance to the war on the poor, especially the trauma-tized families of the incarcerated, the best of struggles. Some advocates are progressive community-based service providers, policy change advocates, or families of prisoner organizations whose mission is to tend to the families wounded by the war on drugs, which has taken so many prisoners. Others fight for an end to the war and the policies of exclusion and inequity that produce it.

ADDENDUM

SUPPORT PROGRAMS FOR FAMILIES
OF INCARCERATED MOTHERS

Aid to Inmate Mothers (AIM)

AIM assists mothers from Tutwiler Prison and their children with reunification and reintegration in the community.

Aid to Inmate Mothers
P.O. Box 985
Montgomery, AL 36104-0985
Telephone: (800) 679-0246 or (334) 262-2245

Assisting Families of Inmates

Inmate Families Organization Inc. (InFO Inc.) provides services, resources, and information to families of offenders; provides information to state officials, the public, and the media concerning the impact the criminal justice system has upon the family members of offenders; helps remove the stigma associated with being family members of offenders through education programs and other support; and assists in the reintegration of families when the offender is released.

Assisting Families of Inmates
1 North 5th Street, Suite 400
Richmond, VA 23219
Telephone: (804) 643-2401
Fax: (804) 643-2464
Linda Reeves's e-mail: infoinc@flash.net

Beyondmedia Education

Beyondmedia Education's mission is to collaborate with underserved and underrepresented women, youth, and communities to tell their stories, connect their stories to the world around us, and organize for social justice through the creation and distribution of alternative media and arts. They partner with community-based organizations and schools in the creation of videos, web sites, exhibitions, handbooks, graphic arts, performances, and public education campaigns.

Beyondmedia Education

7013 N. Glenwood Avenue
Chicago, IL 60626
Telephone: (773) 973-2280
E-mail: beyond@beyondmedia.org

California Coalition for Battered Women in Prison (CCBWP)

Advocacy group for women who have experienced domestic violence. Seeks to contextualize the conditions of women's lives of abuse and to advocate for them in court and during incarceration. Does not deal specifically with children and families of incarcerated mothers.

California Coalition for Battered Women in Prison (CCBWP)

1540 Market Street, Suite 490
San Francisco, CA 94102

Center for Children of Incarcerated Parents

The Center for Children of Incarcerated Parents offers a variety of education and training programs to serve children of offenders and their families. The center offers a variety of correspondence courses nationwide as well as regional courses and training; houses several other programs and research projects working with this population; and has a clearinghouse that distributes publications and audiovisuals both free and at a cost.

Center for Children of Incarcerated Parents

P. O. Box 41-286
Eagle Rock, CA 90041
Telephone: (626) 449-2470
E-mail: ccip@earthlink.net
Website: www.e-ccip.org

Centerforce

Centerforce administers a variety of services for inmates and their families in California facilities, including programs, educational materials, groups, therapy, and case management. Their web site offers links to resources on parenting, substance abuse, youth mentoring programs and services, and support groups. Three ex-prisoners sit on the Centerforce board of directors, and five board members have or had a family member incarcerated. Among Centerforce's staff, 73 percent are either ex-prisoners or have family members who have been incarcerated.

Centerforce
64 Main Street
P.O. Box 336
San Quentin, CA 94964
Telephone: (415) 456-9980
E-mail: info@centerforce.org
Website: www.centerforce.org

Chicago Legal Advocacy to Incarcerated Mothers (CLAIM)

Chicago Legal Advocacy for Incarcerated Mothers provides legal and educational services to help imprisoned mothers preserve their families. Through public advocacy, CLAIM promotes policies and programs to benefit families of imprisoned mothers.

Chicago Legal Advocacy to Incarcerated Mothers (CLAIM)
220 S. State Street, Suite 830
Chicago, IL 60604
Telephone: (312) 675-0911
E-mail: info@c-l-a-i-m.org
Website: www.claim-il.org

Children Made Visible, Inc.

Provides self-help support group, information and referrals.

Children Made Visible, Inc.
P.O. Box 716
Gladstone, OR 97027
Telephone: (503) 699-1388
E-mail: ChildMadeVisible@aol.com
Contact: Mary Ann Colby, Founder/Executive Director

Community Project for Reintegration

Provides legal services and information to formerly incarcerated women.

Community Project for Reintegration
166 Montague Street
Brooklyn, NY 11201
Telephone: (718) 422-2864
E-mail: amcammett@legal-aid.org

Critical Resistance

Advocacy movement challenging the prison-industrial complex as an enterprise of social control that profits from the injustice of targeting and incarcerating the poor, people of color and women. Seeks prison abolition and offers particular focus on the ways in which African-American, Native American, and Latino families are ravaged by penal practices that ignore the collateral damage of incarceration of parents, especially mothers. Directly confronts issues of social inequity and their perpetuation through the prison-industrial complex.

Critical Resistance
1904 Franklin Street, Suite 504
Oakland, CA 94612
Telephone: (510) 444-0484
Fax: (510) 444-2177
E-mail: crnational-AT-criticalresistance.org
Website: www.criticalresistance.org

Families against Mandatory Minimums (FAMM)

Advocacy reform group aimed at challenging mandatory minimum sentences and giving judges the power of discretionary sentencing, which considers both the conditions and degree of transgression and the individual's rehabilitative potential. The group's primary work is educating and advocating for just sentencing.

FAMM
1612 K St., N.W., Suite 700
Washington, D.C. 20006
Telephone: (202) 822-6700
Fax: (202) 822-6704

Families of Prisoners Support Project

Referrals, mentoring, group activities, transportation, family reunification support, public education, and advocacy.

Families of Prisoners Support Group
420 1/2 Gifford Street
Syracuse, NY 13204
Telephone: (315) 475-4822
E-mail: mzender@afsc.org
Website: www.afsc.org
Contact: Luz Marina Zender

Family Justice and La Bodega de la Familia

Community-based storefront program that supports Latino families struggling with drug addiction and/or incarceration issues by building relationships and services that recognize and affirm family and community strengths rather than deficits. Services include counseling and relapse prevention services, walk-in assessment and referral for all neighborhood residents, and 24-hour crisis intervention in drug-related emergencies. La Bodega de la Familia believes that if supported, "families form a first line of defense—and offense—against drug abuse, criminal behavior, and criminal justice system involvement in the lives of poor families. . . . La Bodega has become a model of how to use family resources in the service of justice."

Family Justice and La Bodega de la Familia
272 East Third Street
New York, NY 10009
Telephone: (212) 982-2335
Fax: (212) 982-1765

Family Justice, Inc.

Utilizes family case management, a model that identifies and mobilizes family and community support for the treatment of drug addiction and other criminal justice-related problems. The model is based on La Bodega de la Familia, a storefront program in New York City.

Family Justice, Inc.
272 East Third Street
New York, NY 10009
Telephone: (212) 982-2335

E-mail: cshapiro@familyjusticeinc.org
Website: www.familyjusticeinc.org
Contact: Carol Shapiro, Executive Director

Family Resource Center

The Family Resource Center is a child-friendly family support center located in the New Hampshire Lakes Region coed prison. This joint project of the New Hampshire Department of Corrections and the University of New Hampshire offers seminars that reconnect children and parents, and provides services that can reintegrate families with community networks. Children participate in University of New Hampshire Cooperative Extension 4-H projects with their parents acting in support roles for their children's projects.

The Lakes Region Facility
1 Right Way Path
Laconia, NH 03246
Telephone: (800) 550-0950 (NH) or (603) 528-9265 or 9266
Fax: (603) 528-9273
E-mail: familyresourcecenter@yahoo.com
Program Administrator: Kristina Toth

Family Resource Center

Provides toll-free hotline serving New York State—(800) 344-3314—and a support group.

Family Resource Center

175 Remsen Street, 8th Floor
Brooklyn, NY 11201
Telephone: (800) 344-3314
Website: www.osborneny.org
Contact: Alison Coleman, Coordinator, Family Resource Center
Agency Head: Elizabeth Gaynes, Executive Director, Osborne Association

Family Services of Western Pennsylvania/Families Outside

Provides low-cost transportation, self-help support group, reentry assistance, employment assistance, information, referrals, coping skills, and family videos.

Family Services of Western Pennsylvania/Families Outside

6401 Penn Avenue, 2nd Floor
Pittsburgh, PA 15206

Telephone: (412) 661-1670
Contact: Ned Pfundt, Coordinator
Agency Head: Donald Goughler, CEO

Family Ties

Provides New York City families with transportation to Albion Correctional Facility (the largest women's prison in New York State), which is 400 miles away. Arranges stays for children and their caretakers. Provides post release family reunification support, job training/employment services and drug rehab/health care referrals.

Family Ties

175 Remsen Street, Eighth Floor
Brooklyn, NY 11201
Telephone: (718) 637-6560
Fax: (718) 237-0686
E-mail: info@osborneny.org

Friends Outside in Santa Clara

Forty-year-old Bay Area organization assists family through the crisis of incarceration. Sets up peer support groups for family members, provides recreational and educational programs for children, emphasizes maintenance of family bonds through visitation and provides extensive services to support family reunification upon release.

Friends Outside in Santa Clara

551 Stockton Ave.
San Jose, CA 95126
Telephone: (408) 295-6033
Fax: (408) 295-2907

Grace House

Community-based transition home for women providing support services, employment connections, and child–mother reunification services.

Grace House

1803 W. Adams
Chicago, IL 60612
Telephone: (312) 733-5363
Contact: Mary Dolan, O.P.

Hour Children

Provides a unique continuity of services to New York mothers and children from point of incarceration to postrelease housing and family support services. My Mother's House I is a residential home for the children of incarcerated mothers, which facilitates ongoing weekly prison visitation; Hour Children's House II is a residential transition program for released mothers and their children; Hour Children's House III is a work-release center for mothers and infants who participated in Taconic or Bedford Hills Prison Nursery programs; My Mother's House II is for infants/toddlers whose mothers are incarcerated and families reuniting; and Hour Apartment House I is a program of permanent housing for families who have completed Hour Children's transitional programs.

Hour Children

36-11A 12th St.
Long Island City, NY 11106
Telephone: (718) 433-4724
Fax: (718) 433-4728
E-mail: hour.children@worldnet.att.net
Executive Director: Sr. Tesa Fitzgerald

JusticeWorks Community

Nonprofit advocacy organization for incarcerated women with special attention to the plight of mothers and the fate of their children.

JusticeWorks Community

1012 Eighth Ave.
Brooklyn, NY 11215
Telephone: (718) 499-6704
Fax: (718) 832-2832
Website: www.justiceworks.org

Legal Action Center

Provides legal information for people with criminal records, HIV/AIDS, and drug and alcohol problems.

Legal Action Center

153 Waverly Place, 8th Floor
New York, NY 10014
Telephone: (212) 243-1313

E-mail dmukamal@lac.org
Website: www.lac.org
Contact: Debbie Mukamal, Staff Attorney

Legal Resources and Services for Prisoners with Children (California)

Offers legal service, advocacy, and resources for prisoners who are parents. Excellent info packet that tells parents exactly what rights they have, how to provide for children at time of arrest, and concrete info regarding what is required to keep their parental rights; legislative packet and info on the appeals process in California prisons; list of most recent videos on mothers in the California prison system.

Legal Resources and Services for Prisoners with Children
1540 Market Street, Suite 4090
San Francisco, CA 94102
Telephone: (415) 255-7036
E-mail: info@prisonerswithchildren.org

Legal Services for Prisoners with Children

Class action litigation and legal advocacy/referrals for parents in prison. Provides information on issues of foster care, termination of parental rights, and pregnancy care. No individual legal representation. Publishes *Incarcerated Parents Manual.*

Legal Services for Prisoners with Children
100 McAllister Street
San Francisco CA 94102
Telephone: (415) 255-7036

Motheread, Inc.

Provides curriculum-based training. A variety of Motheread curricula deal with how to develop literacy skills in specific contexts with different populations. A needs assessment process provides the thematic focus. Lessons are then written and field-tested in classroom settings. These curricula are disseminated through specially designed trainings and workshops.

The Motheread Institute teaches how to conduct Motheread/Fatheread classes in which parents improve their own reading skills, help their children become better readers and thinkers, and improve family communication.

The Working with Spanish-Speaking Families Workshop enhances cultural sensitivities, teaches specific instructional strategies, and provides training in curriculum based on bilingual Latino children's literature.

Storysharing Training teaches how to share stories with children ages two to eleven to foster creative thinking and problem-solving skills, nurture a love of books, and aid in the development of comprehension skills.

B.A.B.Y. (Birth and Beginning Years) teaches how to foster health care, parenting, and literacy behaviors with new and expectant parents. Two different supplements relating to substance abuse and adolescent pregnancy are included.

F.a.t.h.e.r. (Fathers Acting to Heal, Educate, and Reconnect) shows how to help incarcerated fathers connect with their children through skill-building and discussion activities.

Local literacy services: A variety of classes serve adults with different reading abilities and prior educational experiences. Professional instruction staff members lead small classes in which students learn not only how to improve their own literacy skills but also how these new skills can help their children and their communities.

National network: Throughout the United States and its territories, Motheread has developed affiliate partnerships with twelve humanities councils. Over 800 instructors are trained annually from family literacy and family support programs nationwide.

Motheread, Inc.
Suite 7, 3924 Browning Place
Raleigh, NC 27609
Telephone: (919) 781-2088
Fax: (919) 571-8579
E-mail: motheread@earthlink.net
Website: www.motheread.org

Mothers Reclaiming Our Children/Equal Rights Congress

Nationwide program of support for mothers in prison who are attempting to keep their families intact; educates, organizes, provides counseling and a hotline for inmates needing info and some legal advice.

Mothers Reclaiming Our Children/Equal Rights Congress
4167 S. Normandies Avenue
Los Angeles, CA 90037

National Clearinghouse for the Defense of Battered Women

Provides information, referrals, technical assistance, public education and advocacy, and legal information and resources.

National Clearinghouse for the Defense of Battered Women
125 South 9th Street, Suite 302
Philadelphia, PA 19107
Telephone: (215) 351-0010
Contact: Sue Osthoff, Director

New Beginnings Even Start

Provides transportation, referrals, family reunification support, and family literacy and advocacy for incarcerated parents, their children and their children's caregivers.

New Beginnings Even Start
28 Canal Street
Lyons, NY 14489
Telephone: (315) 946-7530
Contact: Sue McMaster, Coordinator
Agency Head: Robin Canne, Director

Osborne Association

Family Resource Center Hotline; visitation program for children with mothers in Albion Correctional Facility; drug treatment, health, mental health, and employment assistance.

Osborne Association
135 East 15th Street
New York, NY 10003
Telephone: (212) 673-6633
Website: www.osborneny.org
Contact: Elizabeth Gaynes, Executive Director

Parents and Children Together, Inc.
P.A.C.T. (Texas)

Offers parent seminars, support groups for children, advocates for families, and referral services.

P.A.C.T
2836 Hemphill
Fort Worth, TX 76110
Telephone: (817) 924-7776
E-mail: dkpact@juno.com

ParentWISE, Inc.

Provides parent education, self-help support group, information and referrals.

ParentWISE, Inc.
409 Coulter Avenue, Suite 2
Greensburg, PA 15601
Telephone: (724) 837-5410
E-mail: pwise@a1usa.net
Contact: Terri Katzman, Executive Director

P.E.A.C.E., Inc., Early Head Start

Provides parent education, referrals, family reunification support, case management, and advocacy for pregnant and postpartum women incarcerated in Onondaga County Correctional Center, their children, and their children's caregivers.

P.E.A.C.E., Inc., Early Head Start
808 North McBride Street
Syracuse, NY 13203
Telephone: (315) 470-3371 ext. 316
E-mail: cmeehan@peace-caa.org
Website: www.peace-caa.org
Contact: Coleen A. Meehan, Assistant Director of Child Development
Agency Head: Lisa Alford, Executive Director

Peanut Butter and Jelly/Project ImPACT

Project IMPACT provides inmates a therapeutic visitation program for children, classes for parents, intensive support for transition during a mother's last year in prison, a residential mother and children program with intensive drug rehab and communal support.

Peanut Butter and Jelly/Project ImPACT
1101 Lopez Southwest
Albuquerque, NM 87105
Telephone: (505) 877-7060

Prison Families Anonymous

Provides referrals, case management, mentoring, family reunification, and advocacy.

Prison Families Anonymous
551 Livingston Street
Westbury, NY 11590
Telephone: (516) 616-3191
E-mail: bbarballan@gateway.net
Contact: Barbara Allan, Director
Agency Head: Barbara Treen, Executive Director

Prison Families of New York, Inc.

Provides information, referrals, reunification support, self-help support groups, public information, and advocacy.

Prison Families of New York, Inc.
40 North Main Avenue
Albany, NY 12203
Telephone: (518) 453-6659
E-mail: alison.coleman@rcda.org
Contact: Alison Coleman, Director

Prisoner Visitation and Support

Provides volunteer visitors to prisoners who get no, or few, other visitors.

Prisoner Visitation and Support
1501 Cherry Street
Philadelphia, PA 19102
Telephone: (215) 241-7117
E-mail: pvs@afsc.org
Website: www.prisonervisitation.org
Contact: Eric Carson, Director
Agency Head: Eric Carson, Director

Project Return

Project Return stresses community building, supports transition to community and employment, and assists in reestablishing family community links for former inmates with special attention to those with addictions. Concentrates on those with a high risk of recidivism in order to help them break cycles of reimprisonment/relapse. Over 2,000 adult and youth participants have graduated from the program since 1993. During the first year, the time when most inmates return to crime, the program intervention maintains an 89.3 percent success rate, with only one in ten program graduates returning to crime.

In year one, the recidivism rate for a control group was 37.2 percent; for program graduates it was 10.7 percent. In year two, the failure rate for the control group was 51 percent while for program graduates it was 24.4 percent. Further analysis of the data showed that although 40 percent of all Project Return graduates had originally been convicted of violent crimes, of those graduates who relapsed over a period of four years, only 6 percent did so for violent offenses.

Project Return
2703 General de Gaulle Drive
New Orleans, LA 70114-6222
Telephone: (504) 988-1000
Fax: (504) 988-1019

Re-Connection

Supports women coming out of prison by setting up referrals, and offering employment counseling and other transition resources.

Re-Connection
7315 S. Yale
Chicago, IL 60621
Telephone: (773) 846-3600
E-mail: PatriciaSchlosser@LSSI.org
Contact: Patricia Schlosser, O.F.S.

S.K.I.P., Inc. (Save Kids of Incarcerated Parents) Alabama

Nonprofit that provides community resource services, offers a network of services for children (one month to eighteen years of age) of incarcerated parents that includes: educational programs for parents and children, play therapy, character and career development, Kids Helping Kids peer mentoring program, and SKIP Volunteers and Counseling Services.

S.K.I.P., Inc. (Save Kids of Incarcerated Parents) Alabama
669 Bush Drive
Hope Hull, AL 36043
Telephone: (334) 284-8103
E-mail: skipinc@mindspring.com

Women A.R.I.S.E.—A Day Reporting Center

Women A.R.I.S.E. is a Detroit community-based organization that provides education, support, and training for former and current women inmates. Focuses on diversion from incarceration through alternative sentencing. Does not specifically address children of incarcerated mothers, although there are support services including child care and Head Start opportunities.

Women A.R.I.S.E.
13100 Averhill Court
Detroit, MI 48215
Telephone: (313) 331-1800
Fax: (313) 331-8797
E-mail: womendrc@aol.com

Women at Risk Program

Provides a community-based sentencing alternative for women. Services include referrals, case management, child care, advocacy, and mental health and substance abuse treatment.

Women at Risk Program
P.O. Box 7472
Asheville, NC 28802
Telephone: (828) 252-2485
E-mail: wccj@mindspring.com
Contact: Brenda Carleton, Program Director
Agency Head: Ellen Clarke, Executive Director

Women's Bureau, U.S. Department of Labor

Assistance with postprison employment needs.

Women's Bureau, U.S. Department of Labor
200 Constitution Avenue NW #S3002
Washington, D.C. 20210
Telephone: (202) 219-8913

Women in Prison Project, National Women's Law Center

Legal advocacy for women in the District of Columbia. Published *Vision beyond Survival: A Resource Guide for Incarcerated Women.*

Women in Prison Project, National Women's Law Center
11 Dupont Circle NW #800
Washington, D.C. 20036

Women's Prison Association and Home, Inc.

Extensive advocacy, services and curriculum for families. Services include reunification, community residential placements, legal assistance, and case management.

Publications: *Supporting Women Offenders and Their Families, Family to Family Tools for Rebuilding Foster Care: Partnerships between Corrections and Child Welfare, Breaking the Cycle of Despair: Children of Incarcerated Mothers* (accompanying video available), *The Foster Care Handbook for Incarcerated Parents: A Manual of Your Legal Rights and Responsibilities, Parenting from Inside/Out: the Voices of Mothers in Prison,* and *Introduction to the Child Welfare and Criminal Justice Systems.*

Women's Prison Association and Home, Inc.
110 Second Avenue
New York, NY 10003
Telephone: (212) 674-1163
Website: www.wpaonline.org
Contact: Vicki Zubovic, Director of Development
Agency Head: Ann Jacobs, Executive Director

CORRECTION-BASED PROGRAMS

National

Girl Scouts beyond Bars

The Girl Scouts beyond Bars program is a mother–daughter visitation program that initiates a daughter into a Girl Scout troop. The National Institute of Justice recommends contacting local Girl Scout organizations for updated information. This is a national initiative.

Mother Child Community Corrections Programs/Services/Transition Houses (This is an extensive, national list.)

National Institute of Corrections, Women Offenders survey listing of all states with correctional-affiliated programs that assist women prisoners and mothers with children. List is made available to jurisdictions and organizations wishing to see other state-affiliated models. Some programs are institutionally based and others community based.

National Institute of Corrections, Women Offenders
National Institute of Justice, U.S. Department of Justice
633 Indiana Avenue, N.W., Room 805
Washington, D.C. 20531
Telephone: (202) 514-6205
Website: www.ojp.usdoj.gov/nij/pubs-sum/156217.htm

Neil J. Houston House, Massachusetts Department of Corrections

The Neil J. Houston House is a residential, prerelease, substance abuse treatment program. Administered by Social Justice for Women, Inc., it is a national model offering an alternative to incarceration and mother-infant separation for pregnant, nonviolent offenders and their infants.

Neil J. Houston House
180 Morton Street, 2nd floor
Jamaica Plain, MA 02130
Telephone: (617) 445-3066 or 727-4672
Website: www.state.ma.us/doc/facility/Fcommunity.html

Selection of State Facilities

Indiana

Craine House Residential Community Corrections and Day Reporting Program

Indianapolis family residential and day reporting program for mothers in community corrections custody; in operation for over twenty years. There are approximately six mothers and eleven children in this program collaboratively sponsored by Craine House staff and the Marion County Community Corrections.

Craine House Residential Community Corrections and Day Reporting Program
3535 North Pennsylvania Street
Indianapolis, IN 46205
Telephone: (317) 925-2833
Fax: (317) 925-2834
E-mail: cajustice1@aol.com
Contact: Cheryl Justice, Executive Director

Maine

Project HIP (Helping Incarcerated Parents)

Project HIP supports incarcerated parents, offering support and continuing education groups. A handbook called *Prisoners as Parents: Building Parenting Skills on the Inside* is available from the National Child Welfare Resource Center for Organizational Improvement—(800) HELP KID.

Maine Correctional Center
17 Mallison Road
Windham, ME 04062
Telephone: (207) 892-6716

Michigan

Project Seek (Services to Enable and Empower Kids) Michigan

Michigan Department of Community Health, Departments of Corrections and Social Services program. Wraparound services, emphasis on prevention of disruption of child's school and social life, focus on building strength in entire family.

Project Seek
Mott Children's Health Center
806 Tuuri Place
Flint, MI 48503
Telephone: (810) 767-5750
Fax: (810) 768-7512
Contact: Carol Burton, M.S.W., Coordinator

New York

Children's Center at Bedford Hills Correctional Facility

Children's center offers child-friendly visitation; summer visiting program with children and teens staying with area host families; nursery program that allows mother and infant to remain together for up to eighteen months. Provides legal services/education concerning foster care, custody, family law, child development, and prenatal workshops.

Children's Center at Bedford Hills Correctional Facility
247 Harris Road
Bedford Hills, NY 10507
Telephone: (914) 241-3100 ext. 4050
Website: childrens_center@mindspring.com
Contact: Toni Campoamor, Director

New York State Department of Correctional Services

Provides family counseling and family reunification support through the Transitional Services Program, children's centers in visiting areas, parent education, information, and referrals. The Family Reunion Program provides extended private visits in secure sites on facility grounds.

New York State Department of Correctional Services
1220 Washington Avenue
Albany, NY 12226
Telephone: (518) 457-3525
Contact: Loyce Duke, Statewide Coordinator for Transitional Services

North Carolina

ECO, Inc. (Energy Committed to Offenders, Inc.)

Provides case management, family reunification support, family therapy, a community residential program, public education, advocacy, children's visitation, and employment preparation.

ECO, Inc.
P.O. Box 33533
Charlotte, NC 28233-3533
Telephone: (704) 374-0762
E-mail: ecoclark@infi.net
Contact: Myra M. Clark, Executive Director

M.A.T.C.H. (Mothers and Their Children)

Provides transportation, a child-friendly visiting center, self-help support group, referrals, family reunification support, advocacy for mothers incarcerated at North Carolina Correctional Institution for Women and their children.

M.A.T.C.H.
1034 Bragg Street
Raleigh, NC 27611
Telephone: (919) 828-4767
E-mail: prisonmatch@aol.com
Website: www.prisonmatch.com
Contact: Dianne M. Daniels, Director
Agency Head: Pat Vineitorio, Social Work Supervisor III

Summit House
Child-friendly visiting centers, referrals.

Summit House
122 N. Elm Street, Suite 910
Greensboro, NC 27401
Telephone: (336) 691-9888

Fax: (336) 275-5042 (fax)
Website: www.summithouse.org

Summit House Piedmont
Administrative Office
122 N. Elm Street, Suite 910
Greensboro, NC 27401
Telephone: (336) 275-9366
Fax: (336) 275-5042

Summit House of Charlotte
P. O. Box 37094
Charlotte, NC 28237-7094
Telephone: (704) 334-4423
Fax: (704) 334-9464

Summit House of Raleigh
P. O. Box 27284
Raleigh, NC 27611-7284
Telephone: (919) 755-0733
Fax: (919) 755-9560

Ohio

Allen Correctional Institution

Children's center; provides family literacy program in which inmates read a child's book onto a tape that is then sent to the child.

Allen Correctional Institution
P.O. Box 4501
Lima, OH 45802
Telephone: (419) 224-8000
E-mail: mathew.schweyer@odrc.state.oh.us
Contact: Mathew T. Schweyer, Recovery Service Director
Agency Head: James Haviland, Warden

Chillicothe Correctional Institution

Provides a parent education program.

Chillicothe Correctional Institution
15802 State Route 104 North
Chillicothe, OH 45601
Telephone: (740) 773-2616

Contact: Linda Woods, Case Manager
Agency Head: Michael Randle, Warden

Correctional Reception Center
Aunt Mary's Storybook Project (tapes for children and holiday family events). Parents read a story into a tape recorder, which children then listen to while they read the story.

Correctional Reception Center
P.O. Box 300
Orient, OH 43146
Telephone: (614) 877-2441
E-mail: candy.cain@odrc.state.oh.us
Contact: Candy Cain, Unit Management Administrator
Agency Head: Mark Saunders, Warden

Franklin Pre-Release Center

Provides Aunt Mary's Storybook tapes for children. Head Start program for preschoolers once a week. Girl Scouts mother-daughter/son scouting activities. Ohio Reads program (literacy tutoring). Family Ties provides visiting activities for incarcerated women and their families.

Franklin Pre-Release Center
1800 Harmon Avenue
Columbus, OH 43223
Telephone: (614) 445-8600
Contact: Julie Janson, Parenting Coordinator
Agency Head: Patricia Andrews, Warden

Grafton Correctional Institution

Children's center in visiting area; inmate substance abuse program.

Grafton Correctional Institution
2500 South Avon Belden Road
Grafton, OH 44012
Telephone: (440) 748-1161
Contact: Marsha Niswonger, Unit Management Administrator
Agency Head: Carl S. Anderson, Warden

Lima Correctional Institution

Provides parent education, father–daughter Girl Scout activities, special parent–child visiting, family reunification support, family literacy and audio taping of stories for children.

Lima Correctional Institution

P.O. Box 4571
Lima, OH 45802
Telephone: (419) 225-8060
Contact: Deb Dunnigan, Administrative Assistant
Agency Head: Michael Leonard, Warden

Montgomery Education and Pre-Release Center

Provides children's center in visiting area, parent education, information, referrals, case management, and family reunification support.

Montgomery Education and Pre-Release Center

1901 South Gettysburg Avenue
Dayton, OH 45418
Telephone: (937) 262-9853
Contact: Cambra Mockabee, Correctional Program Specialist
Agency Head: Curtis Wingard, Warden

Noble Correctional Institution

Provides parent education, self-help support group, information, and referrals.

Noble Correctional Institution

15708 State Route 78W
Caldwell, OH 43724
Telephone: (740) 732-5188
Contact: Tim Buchanan, Unit Management Administrator
Agency Head: Jeff Wolfe, Warden

North Central Correctional Institution

Provides Aunt Mary's Storybook, where inmates read storybooks on audiocassettes, which are then sent to their children and/or grandchildren; and GOAL (Gaining Opportunity in Living Skills) program teaches positive motivational skills. Inmates take the class while their children in Hamilton County participate in the same program. Several times the children visit for a portion of the program.

North Central Correctional Institution
670 Marion-Williamsport Road-E
Marion, OH 43301
Telephone: (740) 387-7040
Contact: Brian P. Byorth, Unit Management Administrator
Agency Head: John D. Morgan, Ward

Ohio Reformatory for Women (ORW)

Provides the following programs: Camp Adventure Mom and Me, Child Support Seminar, Family Day, Responsible Family Life Skills, Strengthening Family Ties, Parents Anonymous, ORW Nursery Program, Mom and Kids Day, Camp Adventure, Aunt Mary's Storybook, Angel Tree, and 4-H Program.

Ohio Reformatory for Women
1479 Collins Avenue
Marysville, OH 43040
Telephone: (937) 642-1065
Contact: Betsey Johnson, Program Coordinator
Agency Head: D. Timmerman-Cooper, Warden

Pickaway Correctional Institution

Provides parent education, children's center in visiting area, information, and referrals.

Pickaway Correctional Institution
P.O. Box 209
Orient, OH 43146
Telephone: (614) 877-4362
E-mail: orc-noblej@ohio.gov
Website: www.drc.state.oh.us
Contact: Jeffrey B. Noble, Unit Management Administrator

Wilmington College—Franklin Pre-Release Center

Provides enhanced visiting, self-help support group, information, and referrals in a community residential program.

Wilmington College—Franklin Pre-Release Center
1800 Harmon Avenue
Columbus, OH 43031
Telephone: (614) 445-8600 ext. 2218
Contact: G. Tammy Riffe, Prenatal Coordinator

Oklahoma

Tulsa Parenting Partnership

Provides transportation, children's center in visiting area, parent education, self-help support group, information and referrals, case management, group activities for children, family reunification support, and family therapy.

Tulsa Parenting Partnership
1608 South Elwood
Tulsa, OK 74119
Telephone: (918) 587-3888
Contact: Mae Ann Shepherd, Executive Director

Oregon

ADAPT

Provides transportation, information and referrals, case management, gifts for children, and family reunification support.

ADAPT
421 SW Fifth Avenue, Suite 700
Portland, OR 97204
Telephone: (503) 988-3747
E-mail: cathryn.a.heron@co.multnomah.or.us
Contact: Cathryn Heron, Corrections Counselor

Eastern Oregon Correctional Institution

Provides parent education.

Eastern Oregon Correctional Facility
2500 Westgate
Pendleton, OR 97801
Telephone: (541) 276-0700 ext. 524
E-mail: jacker@bmcc.cc.or.us
Contact: Jan Acker, Parenting Instructor

Family Intervention Strategic Initiative

Provides information and referrals.

Family Intervention Strategic Initiative
421 SW Fifth Avenue, Suite 700
Portland, OR 97204

Telephone: (503) 988-3136 ext. 27396
E-mail: robert.j.trachtenberg@co.multnomah.or.us
Website: www.co.multnomah.or.us/dcj/tsfamilyinterservices.html
Contact: Robert Trachtenberg, Family Intervention Coordinator

Juvenile Division—Multnomah County Department of Community Justice

Provides parent education, self-help support group, information and referrals, child care, family reunification support, and family therapy for adult parolees and their adolescent children.

Juvenile Division—Multnomah County Department of Community Justice
1401 NE 68th Street
Portland, OR 97213
Telephone: (503) 988-3460
E-mail: elsie.m.garland@co.multnomah.or.us
Website: www.multnomah.lib.or.us/
Contact: Elsie M. Garland, Juvenile Court Counselor-Program Coordinator

Pennsylvania

18th Street Development Corporation/Raising Others' Children

Provides parent education, self-help support group, information and referrals, case management, and mentoring for caregivers raising children who are not their own.

18th Street Development Corporation/Raising Others' Children
1815 South 18th Street
Philadelphia, PA 19145
Telephone: (215) 271-0052
Contact: Sherra Dunn, Director of Family Services
Agency Head: Elizabeth Burns, Executive Director of ESDC

Bethesda Family Services Foundation

Provides parent education, self-help support group, information and referrals, religious ministry (if requested), family reunification support, and family therapy.

Publications: *Foster Care Program Description*, $10.00; *Family Systems Model*, $10.00; *Parenting Program Overview*, $10.00; *Bad Dads* (video), $15.00.

Bethesda Family Services Foundation
P.O. Box 210
West Milton, PA 17886
Telephone: (570) 568-2373
E-mail: staff@bfsf.org
Website: www.bfsf.org
Contact: Jim Dressler, Parenting Program Coordinator
Agency Head: Dominic Herbst, President

Pennsylvania Department of Corrections

Provides transportation, children's centers in visiting areas, parent education, self-help support groups, gifts for children, family reunification support, and family therapy at various Pennsylvania facilities.

Pennsylvania Department of Corrections
2520 Lisburn Road
Camp Hill, PA 17001-0598
Telephone: (717) 730-2715
E-mail: jabell@state.pa.us
Contact: James H. Bell, Pardons Case Specialist/Family Services

SCI—Muncy

Provides transportation, children's center in visiting area, enhanced visiting, parent education, self-help support group, information, referrals, gifts for children, family reunification support, and public education and advocacy.

SCI—Muncy
P.O. Box 180
Muncy, PA 17754
Telephone: (570) 546-3171
Contact: Melinda A. Smith, Parenting Program Director
Agency Head: Donald L. Kelchner, Superintendent

NOTES

INTRODUCTION

1. Katherine Gabel and Denise Johnston, *Children of Incarcerated Parents* (New York: Lexington Books, 1995).
2. Mechtild Hart, *The Poverty of Life-Affirming Work: Motherwork, Education and Social Change* (Westport, CT: Greenwood Press, 2002), 13.
3. Ruth Behar, *The Vulnerable Observer* (Boston, MA: Beacon Press, 1996), 7.
4. Behar, 9.
5. Katherine Gabel and Denise Johnston, "Incarcerated Parents," in *Children of Incarcerated Parents*, eds. Katherine Gabel and Denise Johnston (New York: Lexington Books, 1995), 10; Christopher Mumola, "Incarcerated Parents and Their Children," U.S. Department of Justice, Bureau of Justice Statistics Special Report (Washington, D.C.: U.S. Government Printing Office, 2000), 9.
6. bell hooks, *Yearning: Race, Gender, and Cultural Politics* (Boston: South End Press, 1990).

CHAPTER 1

1. Nicole Hahn Rafter, *Creating Born Criminals* (Chicago: University of Illinois Press, 1997), 238.
2. U.S. Department of Justice, Bureau of Justice Statistics, "Prisoners in 1998" (Washington, D.C.: U.S. Government Printing Office, August 1999).
3. Laurence Greenfield and Tracy Snell, "Women Offenders," U.S. Department of Justice, Bureau of Justice Statistics (Washington, D.C.: U.S. Government Printing Office, 1999), 7.
4. Christian Parenti, *Lockdown America* (New York: Verso, 1999), 58.
5. Michel Foucault, *Discipline and Punishment: The Birth of the Prison* (New York: Pantheon, 1977), 9.
6. Christopher Mumola, "Incarcerated Parents and Their Children," U.S. Department of Justice, Bureau of Justice Statistics Special Report (Washington, D.C.: U.S. Government Printing Office, 2000), 1.
7. Monique Hoefinger, Review of *All Too Familiar: Sexual Abuse of Women in U.S. State Prisons*, *Human Rights Quarterly* 21, no. 1 (1999): 254–59.

8. Stephanie Bush-Baskette, "The War on Drugs, a War Against Women?," in *Harsh Punishment: International Experiences of Women's Imprisonment*, eds. Sandy Cook and Suzanne Davies (Boston, MA: Northeastern University, 1999), 222.
9. Mumola, 2.
10. Tracy Snell, "Women in Prison," U.S. Department of Justice, Bureau of Justice Statistics Special Report (Washington, D.C.: U.S. Government Printing Office, 1991), 1.
11. Mumola, 2.
12. Mumola, 2.
13. Bush-Baskette, 221.
14. Greenfield and Snell, 1.
15. Bush-Baskette, 215.
16. Jeffrey Reiman, *The Rich Get Richer and the Poor Get Prison* (Boston: Allyn & Bacon, 2001), 121.
17. Steve Donzinger, ed., *The Real War on Crime: The Report of the National Criminal Justice Commission* (New York: HarperPerennial, 1996), 120.
18. Mumola, 3.
19. Donzinger, 150.
20. Mumola, 9.
21. Katherine Gabel and Denise Johnston, "Incarcerated Parents," in *Children of Incarcerated Parents*, eds. Katherine Gabel and Denise Johnston (New York: Lexington, 1995), 10.
22. Greenfield and Snell, 1.
23. Suzanne Rostler, "Study Shows Link between Child Abuse, Drugs," Reuters Health, January 7, 2002, http://preventdisease.com/news/articles/link_child_abuse_drugs.shtml (accessed June 21, 2005).
24. Ibid.
25. Ralph Nunez, *A Tale of Two Nations: The Creation of "American Poverty Nomads"* (New York: Homes for the Homeless, January 1996), 259.
26. Children's Defense Fund, "High Cost of Child Care Puts Quality Care out of Reach of Many Families," Press Release, December 11, 2000.
27. Children's Defense Fund, *Child Care Basics Fact Sheet* (Washington, D.C.: Children's Defense Fund, 2000), citing Amara Bachau and Martin O'Connell, *Current Population Reports: Fertility of American Women* (Washington, D.C.: U.S. Bureau of the Census, 2000).
28. Children's Defense Fund, "Hardship Faced by Low Income Working Families Who Have Left Welfare since 1996," Press Release, December 14, 2000.
29. Nina Bernstein, "Medicaid Rolls Have Declined in the Last Three Years," *New York Times*, August 17, 1998, B1.

CHAPTER 2

1. Kum-Kum Bhavani and Angela Davis, "Women in Prison: Researching Race in Three National Contexts," in *The Criminal Justice System and Women*, eds. Barbara R. Price and Natalie Sokoloff (New York: McGraw-Hill, 2004), 208.
2. Nancy Campbell, *Using Women: Gender, Drug Policy and Social Justice* (New York: Routledge, 2000), 201.
3. Ann Russo, *Taking Back Our Lives* (New York: Routledge, 2001), 1.
4. Paul Street, "Marriage as the Solution to Poverty," *Z*, April 2002, 34.
5. Street, 34.
6. Street, 34.
7. Street, 33.

8. Sheila Collins and Gertrude Schaffner Goldberg, *Washington's New Law: Welfare Reform and the Road Not Taken, 1935 to the Present* (New York: Apex Press, 2001), 11.

9. Southwest Youth Collaborative, *Zero Tolerance: Resisting the Drive for Punishment in Our Schools* (Chicago: Southwest Youth Collaborative Publications, 2001).

10. Street, 35.

11. Street, 37.

12. Campbell, 168.

13. Beth Ritchie, *Compelled to Crime: The Gender Entrapment of Battered Black Women* (New York: Routledge, 1996).

14. Dorothy Roberts, *Killing the Black Body* (New York: Pantheon, 1997), 24.

15. Daniel Neuspiel, "Racism and Pre-Natal Addiction," *Ethnicity and Disease*, no. 6 (1996): 47–55; Ira Chasnoff, Harold Landress, and Anna M. Barrett, "The Prevalence of Illicit Drug or Alcohol Use during Pregnancy and Discrepancies in Mandatory Reporting in Pinellas County, Florida," *New England Journal of Medicine*, no. 17 (1990): 1202–6.

16. Roberts, 153.

17. Roberts, 157.

18. Deborah Frank et al., "Growth, Development, Behavior in Early Childhood Following Pre-Natal Cocaine Exposure: A Systematic Review," *Journal of American Medical Association*, March 28, 2001, 1613–1625.

CHAPTER 3

1. Lynn Paltrow, "The War on Drugs and the War on Abortion," in *The Criminal Justice System and Women*, eds. Barbara R. Price and Natalie Sokoloff (New York: McGraw-Hill, 2004), 176.

2. Beth Ritchie, *Compelled to Crime: The Gender Entrapment of Battered Black Women* (New York: Routledge, 1996), 5.

CHAPTER 4

1. Kathy Nolan, O.P., interview with the author, December 21, 2002.

2. Katherine Gabel and Denise Johnston, "Incarcerated Parents," in *Children of Incarcerated Parents*, eds. Katherine Gabel and Denise Johnston (New York: Lexington Books, 1995), 10.

3. Gabel and Johnston, "Incarcerated Parents," 10.

4. Christopher Mumola, "Incarcerated Parents and Their Children," U.S. Department of Justice, Bureau of Justice Statistics Special Report (Washington, D.C.: U.S. Government Printing Office, 2000), 9.

5. Patricia Schlosser, O.F.S., interview with the author, December 17, 2001.

6. Katherine Gabel and Denise Johnston, "Effects of Parental Incarceration," in *Children of Incarcerated Parents* (New York: Lexington Books, 1995), 80.

7. Schlosser interview.

8. Philip Genty, "Termination of Parental Rights" in *Children of Incarcerated Parents*, eds. Katherine Gabel and Denise Johnston (New York: Lexington Books, 1995), 169.

9. Gabel and Johnston, "Incarcerated Parents," 16.

10. Nolan interview.

11. Gail Smith, "Practical Considerations," in *Children of Incarcerated Parents*, eds. Katherine Gabel and Denise Johnston (New York: Lexington Books, 1995), 189.

12. Smith, "Practical Considerations," 188.

13. Genty, "Termination of Parental Rights," 168.

14. Nolan interview.
15. Gabel and Johnston, "Incarcerated Parents," 14.
16. Mumola, 1.
17. Mumola, 1.
18. Schlosser interview.
19. Schlosser interview.

CHAPTER 5

1. Joy James, *Resisting State Violence, Radicalism, Gender and Race in U.S. Culture,* (Minneapolis: University of Minnesota Press, 1996), 25–26.
2. Andrew Hacker, *Two Nations: Black and White, Separate, Hostile, Unequal* (New York: Scribner, 2003), 64.
3. Christopher Mumola, "Substance Abuse and Treatment, State and Federal Prisoners," U.S. Department of Justice, Bureau of Justice Statistics (Washington, D.C.: U.S. Government Printing Office, January 1999), 2.
4. Marc Mauer and Tracy Hulling, *Young Black Americans and the Criminal Justice System; Five Years Later* (Washington, D.C.: The Sentencing Project), 20.
5. Institute of Medicine, "Preventing Low Birth Weight Summary (1985)," quoted in Barry Zuckerman, *Drug Exposed Infants: Understanding the Medical Risk*, Center for the Future of Children Report, Woodrow Wilson School of Public and International Affairs at Princeton University and the Brookings Institute (spring 1991).
6. Nancy Campbell, *Using Women: Gender, Drug Policy, and Social Justice* (New York: Routledge, 2000), 6.
7. Dorothy Roberts, *Killing the Black Body: Race, Reproduction and the Meaning of Liberty* (New York: Pantheon, 1997), 159.
8. Amnesty International, "Rights for All: Violations of Women's Rights in Custody," AIUSA Fact Sheet (Washington, D.C.: Amnesty International Publications, 1998), 2.
9. Sarah Karp, "Crack Babies: Black Children Defy Stereotypes, Face Bias," *Chicago Reporter*, February 2001, 2.
10. Karp, 1.
11. Christopher Mumola, "Incacerated Parents and Their Children," U.S. Department of Justice, Bureau of Justice Statistics Special Report (Washington, D.C.: U.S. Government Printing Office, August 2000), 1.
12. Beth Ritchie, *Compelled to Crime: The Gender Entrapment of Battered Black Women* (New York: Routledge, 1996), 14.
13. James, 16.
14. James, 16.
15. Ritchie.
16. The Sentencing Project, "Crack Cocaine Sentencing Policy: Unjustified and Unreasonable," The Sentencing Project Briefing Sheet (Washington, D.C.: Sentencing Project, 2001), 2.
17. Barbara Meierhoefer, "The General Effect of Mandatory Minimum Prison Terms: A Longitudinal Study of Federal Offenses Imposed," Federal Judicial Center Study (Washington, D.C.: Federal Judicial Center, 1992).
18. The Sentencing Project, 2.
19. Karp, 5.
20. D. R. Neuspiel, "Racism and Pre-Natal Addiction," in *Ethnicity and Disease* 6 (1996): 47–55; and Ira Chasnoff et al., "The Prevalence of Illicit Drug Use During Pregnancies and Discrepancies in Mandatory Reporting in Pinellas County Florida," *New England Journal of Medicine*, no. 322 (1990): 1202–6.

21. Florita Z. Louis de Malave, "Sterilization of Puerto Rican Women: A Selected Partially Annotated Bibliography," paper (Madison: University of Wisconsin, 1999), p. 1.
22. American Civil Liberties Union, "Norplant: A New Contraceptive with the Potential for Abuse," ACLU Paper on Reproductive Freedom, January 31, 1994.
23. Children's Defense Fund, "Every Day in America," Children's Defense Fund Report (Washington, D.C.: Children's Defense Fund, 2002), 2–3.
24. Sunhwa Lee et al., "Disabilities among Children and Mothers in Low Income Families," Institute for Women's Policy Research Study (Washington, D.C.: Institute for Women's Policy Research Publications, June 20, 2002), 5.
25. Lee et al., 5.
26. "Life Sentences: Denying Welfare Benefits to Women Convicted of Drug Offenses," The Sentencing Project Fact Sheet (Washington, D.C.: The Sentencing Project, 2002), 1.
27. Patricia Schlosser, O.S.F., interview with the author, December 17, 2001.
28. Noel Cazenave and Kenneth Neubeck, Welfare Racism: Playing the Race Card against America's Poor (New York: Routledge, 2001), 212, 221.
29. Cazenave and Neubeck, 30.
30. Cazenave and Neubeck, 30–31.
31. Cazenave and Neubeck, 31.
32. Valerie Polakow, "Savage Policies: Systemic Violence and the Lives of Children," in The Public Assault on Children: Poverty, Violence and the Juvenile Justice System, ed. Valerie Polakow (New York: Teacher's College, Columbia University, 2000), 1–15.
33. David Pfeiffer, "Eugenics and Disability Discrimination," Disability and Society 9, no. 4 (1994): 481–99.
34. Roberts, 305.
35. James, 119.
36. Christian Parenti, Lockdown America: Police and Prisons in the Age of Crisis (New York: Verso, 1999), 169.

CHAPTER 6

1. Theater of terror is a term coined by Mark Lewis Taylor in The Executed God: The Way of the Cross in Lockdown America (Minneapolis, MN: Fortress Press, 2001); see also Christian Parenti, Lockdown America: Police and Prisons in the Age of Crisis (New York: Verso, 1999).
2. Taylor, 48–49.
3. Mary Koss et al., No Safe Haven: Male Violence against Women at Work, and in the Community (Washington, D.C.: American Psychological Association, 1994), 44.
4. Callie Marie Rennison, "Rape and Sexual Assault: Reports to Police and Medical Attention, 1992–2000," U.S. Department of Justice, Bureau of Justice Statistics (Washington, D.C.: U.S. Government Printing Office, 2000), 1.
5. Human Rights Watch, All Too Familiar: Sexual Abuse of Women in United States Prisons (Washington, D.C.: Human Rights Watch Publications, 1996), Summary, 1.
6. Human Rights Watch, Nowhere to Hide: Retaliation against Women in Michigan State Prisons (Washington, D.C.: Human Rights Publications, 1999), Summary, 4.
7. Human Rights Watch, Nowhere to Hide, Summary, 4.
8. Human Rights Watch, All Too Familiar.
9. Laurence Greenfield and Tracy Snell, "Women Offenders," U.S. Department of Justice, Bureau of Justice Statistics Special Report (U.S. Government Printing Office, 1999), 1.
10. Human Rights Watch, Nowhere to Hide, Summary, 2.
11. Human Rights Watch, Nowhere to Hide, Summary, 3.
12. Human Rights Watch, All Too Familiar, Summary, 2.
13. Human Rights Watch, All Too Familiar, Summary, 2.

14. "Rights for All: Violations of the Human Rights of Women in Custody," Amnesty International Fact Sheet (New York: Amnesty International Publications, 1998), 2 (www.amnestyusa.org/rightsforall/women/factsheets/discrimination.html)
15. Human Rights Watch, *Nowhere to Hide*, Summary, 5.
16. American Civil Liberties Union, "Male Correctional Officers Should Be Restricted from Some Areas of Women's Prisons, ACLU Says," ACLU Press Release, March 6, 2001, 1.
17. Human Rights Watch, *All Too Familiar*, Summary, 5, 6.
18. American Civil Liberties Union, "ACLU Sues Private Prisoner Transport Company over Sexual Assault and Death Threats against Women," ACLU Press Release, April 11, 2001, 1.
19. Amnesty International, "Rights for All," 1.
20. Amnesty International, *United States of America: Rights for All* (New York: Amnesty International Publications, 1998), 70.
21. Amnesty International, "Rights for All," 1.
22. Luana Ross, *Inventing the Savage: The Social Construction of Native American Criminality* (Austin: University of Texas Press, 1998), 194.
23. "Death behind Bars," *San Francisco Bay Guardian*, February 5, 1997, 1.
24. "Death behind Bars," *San Francisco Bay Guardian*, February 5, 1997, 1.
25. Amnesty International, Medical Neglect of Women in U.S. Prisons, in "Rights for All," 1.
26. Ibid., 1.

CHAPTER 7

1. James Baldwin, "Fly in the Buttermilk," in *Experiencing Race, Class, and Gender in the United States*, ed. Virginia Cyrus (Mountain View, CA: Mayfield Publishing, 1993), 431.
2. Hannah Arendt, *On Violence* (New York: Harcourt Brace, 1970), 63.
3. Kathy Nolan, interview with the author, December 21, 2002.
4. June Jordan, *On Call: Political Essays* (Boston: South End Press, 1985), 26.
5. bell hooks, *All About Love* (New York: William Morrow and Company, 2000), xvii, xix, xxix.
6. Rhonda Hammer, *Antifeminism and Family Terrorism: A Critical Perspective* (New York: Rowman and Littlefield Publishers, 2002), 200.
7. Nancy Campbell, *Using Women: Gender, Drug Policy, and Social Justice* (New York: Routledge, 2000), 217.
8. bell hooks, *Yearning: Race, Gender and Cultural Politics* (Boston: South End Press, 1990), 130.

CHAPTER 8

1. Paul Farmer, *Pathologies of Power* (Berkeley: University of California, 2003), 144.
2. bell hooks, *Feminism Is for Everybody: Passionate Politics* (Cambridge, MA: South End Press, 2000), 64.
3. Nancy Campbell, *Using Women: Gender, Drug Policy, and Social Justice* (New York: Routledge, 2000), 6.
4. Michael Harrington, *The Other America: Poverty in the United States* (New York: Penguin, 1971).
5. Joseph Vorassi and James Garbarino, "Poverty and Youth Violence: Not All Risk Factors Are Created Equal," in *The Public Assault on America's Children: Poverty, Violence and Juvenile Injustice*, ed. Valerie Polakow (New York: Teacher's College Press), 61.
6. Vorassi and Garbarino, 61.

7. Children's Defense Fund, "Twenty-five Key Facts about American Children," in *The State of America's Children Yearbook 2001* (Washington, D.C.: Children's Defense Fund, 2001), (www.childrensdefense.org/factsfigures_america.htm).

8. Children's Defense Fund, *Basic Facts on Poverty, Frequently Asked Questions* (Washington, D.C.: Children's Defense Fund, 2001), 1.

9. Beth Ritchie, *Compelled to Crime: The Gender Entrapment of Battered Black Women* (New York: Routledge, 1996).

10. Laurence Greenfield and Tracy Snell, "Women Offenders," U.S. Department of Justice, Bureau of Justice Statistics (Washington, D.C.: U.S. Government Printing Office, 1999), 1.

11. *Too Much: A Quarterly Commentary on Capping Excessive Wealth,* spring 1995, 8.

12. David Betson and Robert Michael, "Why So Many Children Are Poor," *Children and Poverty* 7, no. 2 (summer/fall 1997): 25.

13. Children's Defense Fund, "Overall Child Poverty Rate Dropped in 2000 but Poverty Rose for Children in Full-Time Working Families," Press Release, September 5, 2001.

14. Children's Defense Fund, "Where America Stands," in *The State of America's Children Yearbook 2001,* xi–xxvi.

15. Children's Defense Fund, *The State of Children in America's Union: A 2002 Action Guide to Leave No Child Behind* (Washington, D.C.: Children's Defense Fund, 2002), v.

16. Marian Wright Edelman, "Number of Poor Children in America Rises for the First Time in Eight Years," Children's Defense Fund Press Release (Washington, D.C.: Children's Defense Fund, February 24, 2002).

17. Children's Defense Fund, "Where America Stands," xxi–xxvi.

18. Children's Defense Fund, *Basic Facts on Poverty,* 2.

19. Dorothy Roberts, *Killing the Black Body: Race, Reproduction and the Meaning of Liberty* (New York: Pantheon, 1997), 179, 185.

20. Sue Brooks, "Poverty and Environmentally Induced Damage to Children," in *The Public Assault on America's Children: Poverty, Violence and Juvenile Injustice,* ed. Valerie Polakow (New York: Teacher's College Press, 2000), 45.

21. Brooks, 50, 52.

22. Children's Defense Fund, *The State of Children in America's Union,* iv.

23. Children's Defense Fund, *The State of Children in America's Union,* iv.

24. Deanna Lyter et al., "Children in Single Parent Families Living in Poverty Have Fewer Supports after Welfare," Institute for Women's Policy Research (Washington, D.C.: Institute for Women's Policy Research Publications, 2002), 4, 5.

25. Children's Defense Fund, "Child Care Basics," Children's Defense Fund Report (Washington, D.C.: Children's Defense Fund, 2001), 1.

26. Children's Defense Fund, "Children's Defense Fund Report Finds the High Cost of Child Care Puts Quality Care Out of Reach for Many Families," Children's Defense Fund Report (Washington, D.C.: Children's Defense Fund, 2002), 1.

27. Children's Defense Fund, "Children's Defense Fund Report Finds," 1.

28. Children's Defense Fund, "New Report on Hardships Faced by Low Income Working Families Who Have Left Welfare Since 1996," Children's Defense Fund Press Release Archive, December 14, 2000, 1.

29. Helene Slessarev, *The Betrayal of the Urban Poor* (Philadelphia, PA: Temple University Press, 1997), 6.

30. Patricia Hill Collins, *Black Feminist Thought: Knowledge, Consciousness and Empowerment* (New York: Routledge, 2000).

31. Marc Mauer, *Race to Incarcerate* (New York: The New Press, 1999), 11.

32. Mauer, 9.

33. Amnesty International USA, *United States of America Rights for All* (New York: Amnesty International Publications, 1998), 85, 90.

34. Amnesty International, 89.
35. Amnesty International, 92.
36. Amnesty International, 95.
37. Cazenave and Neubeck, 149.
38. Cazenave and Neubeck, 30.
39. Roberts, *Killing the Black Body.*
40. Marc Mauer, "The Racial Dynamics of Imprisonment," in *Building Violence,* ed. John May (Thousand Oaks, CA: Sage Publications, 2000), 47.
41. Michel Foucault, *Discipline and Punishment: The Birth of the Prison* (New York: Vintage Books, 1979).
42. Noel Cazenave and Kenneth Neubeck, *Welfare Racism: Playing the Race Card against America's Poor* (New York: Routledge), 148.
43. Mark Lewis Taylor, *The Executed God: The Way of the Cross in Lockdown America* (Minneapolis, MN: Fortress Press, 2001), 41–42.
44. Jonathan Kozol, *Savage Inequalities: Children in America's Schools* (New York: Harper-Perennial, 1992).

CHAPTER 9

1. Pamela Thomas, "Inside the Storm," in *Find Her, Feel Her, Free Her Workbook: A Self-Help Guide for the Woman in You* (Chicago, IL: Training Manual for Female Ex-Offenders, 2002), 34.
2. Steven Spritzer, "Toward a Marxist Theory of Deviance," *Social Problems* 22 (1975): 638–51.
3. Thomas, "If I Had Known," 99.
4. Thomas, "If I Had Known," 99.
5. Mark Lewis Taylor, *The Executed God: The Way of the Cross in Lockdown America* (Minneapolis, MN: Fortress Press, 2001).
6. Taylor, 100.
7. Thomas, "If I Had Known," 99.
8. Taylor, 116, 161.
9. Thomas, "If I Had Known," 98.
10. Taylor, 156.
11. Taylor, 113.
12. Pamela Thomas, *Only Women Bleed,* a theater piece, fall 2002.
13. Mariln Frye, "Oppression," in *Feminist Frontiers,* ed. Laurel Richardson et al. (New York: McGraw-Hill, 2001), 7.
14. bell hooks, "Selling Hot Pussy: Representations of Black Female Sexuality in the Cultural Marketplace," in *Feminist Frontiers,* ed. Laurel Richardson et al., 136.
15. Augusto Boal, *Theater of the Oppressed* (New York: Routledge, 1982).

CHAPTER 10

1. Kum Kum Bhavani and Angela Davis, "Women in Prison: Researching Race in Three National Contexts," in *The Criminal Justice System and Women,* eds. Barbara R. Price and Natalie Sokoloff (New York: McGraw-Hill, 2004), 210.
2. Howard Zinn, *You Can't Be Neutral on a Moving Train: A Personal History of Our Times* (Boston, MA: Beacon Press, 2002), x.
3. Joy James, *Resisting State Violence: Radicalism, Gender and Race in U.S. Culture* (Minneapolis: University of Minnesota Press, 1996), 3.
4. James, 4.

5. James, 4.
6. Patricia Hill Collins, *Fighting Words: Black Women and the Search for Justice* (Minneapolis: University of Minnesota Press, 1998), 248.
7. Laureen Snider, "Feminism, Punishment and the Potential of Empowerment," in *Criminology at the Crossroads: Feminist Readings in Crime and Justice*, eds. Kathleen Daly and Lisa Maher (New York: Oxford University Press, 1998), 247.
8. Nina Siegal, "Stopping Abuse in Prison," in *Criminal Justice System and Women*, eds. Price and Sokoloff, 276–77.
9. Siegal, 277–78.
10. Snider, 254.
11. Karlene Faith, "Progressive Rhetoric, Regressive Policies: Canadian Prisons for Women," in *Criminal Justice System and Women*, eds. Price and Sokoloff, 282–86.
12. Faith, 281.
13. Faith, 286.
14. Faith, 285–86.
15. Howard Zehr, *Changing Lenses: A New Focus for Crime and Justice* (Scottdale, PA: Herald Press, 1990).
16. Howard Zehr, *The Little Book of Restorative Justice* (Intercourse, PA: Good Books, 2002).
17. M. Umbriet, R. Coates, and B. Voss, "The Impact of Restorative Justice Conferencing: A Review of 63 Empirical Studies in 5 Countries," (paper) (Minneapolis, MN: Center for Restorative Justice and Peacemaking, 2002), 22.
18. Office of Juvenile Justice and Delinquency Prevention, "The Balanced and Restorative Justice Project," U.S. Department of Justice (Washington, D.C.: U.S. Government Printing Office, 1996), 97.
19. Bruce Arrigo, Dragan Milovanovic, and Robert Schehr, *The French Connection in Criminology: Rediscovering Crime, Law and Social Change* (New York: State University of New York Press), 2005, 101–102.
20. Arrigo et al., 101.
21. Arrigo et al., 104.
22. Zehr, *The Little Book of Restorative Justice*, 14.
23. Karlene Faith, "Seeking Transformative Justice for Women: Views from Canada," *Journal of International Women's Studies*, Vol. 2, no. 1, November 2000.
24. Zehr, *The Little Book of Transformative Justice*, 30.
25. Zehr, *The Little Book of Transformative Justice*, 13.
26. Schehr in Arrigo et al.
27. Richard Parker, "From Conquistador to Corporations," *Sojourner* (May–June 2002), 24.
28. Julie Sudbury, "Women of Color, Globalization, and the Politics of Incarceration," in *The Criminal Justice System and Women*, eds. Price and Sokoloff, 230.
29. Sudbury, 230.
30. Sudbury.
31. Neil Websdale and Meda Chesney-Lind, "Doing Violence to Women: Research Synthesis on the Victimization of Women," in *The Criminal Justice System and Women*, eds. Price and Sokoloff, 305.

CHAPTER 11

1. Robert Drinan, "Winning a Magna Carta for Children," *National Catholic Reporter*, September 26, 2003.
2. Joanne Archibald, "Governor Ryan Signs Pilot Program for Mothers into Law," CLAIM Newsletter, fall 2002, 2.
3. JusticeWorks Community, "Women of Substance: A Drug Abuse Education Project," paper (New York: JusticeWorks Community, 2002), 2–3.

4. Diana Delgado, interview with author, March 2004.
5. Diana Delgado, "Diana Survives, Strives and Testifies," CLAIM Newsletter, fall 2002, 2.
6. Delgado, CLAIM Newsletter, 2–3.
7. Delgado interview.
8. J. D. Wooldredge and K. Masters, "Confronting Problems Faced by Pregnant Inmates in State Prisons," *Crime and Delinquency*, no. 39 (1993): 195–203.
9. "The Children's Center Programs," paper (New York: Bedford Hills Women's Prison, 2004), 1–20.
10. Diane Daane, "Pregnant Prisoners: Health, Security and Special Needs Issues," in *The Incarcerated Woman: Rehabilitative Programming in Women's Prisons*, eds. Susan Sharp and Roslyn Muraskin (Upper Saddle River, NJ: Prentice Hall, 2003), 70.
11. Merry Morash and Pamela Schram, *The Prison Experience: Special Issues of Women in Prison* (Prospect Heights, IL: Waveland Press, 2002), 98.
12. Samir Goswami and Anice Schervish, "Unlocking Options for Women: A Survey of Women in Cook County Jail," The Facts Behind the Faces, Chicago Coalition for the Homeless Policy Paper, spring 2002, 1.
13. Kathy Nolan, O.P., Beyond Media Women in Prison Panel, Chicago, March 25, 2004.
14. "Barriers to Re-entry," *WPA (Women's Prison Association) Focus on Women and Justice Newsletter*, October 2003.
15. Barbara Ehrenreich and Frances Fox Piven, "Without a Safety Net," *Mother Jones*, May, June 2002, 36.
16. Mark Greenberg, "TANF and Criminal Convictions," paper presented at the National Legal Aid and Defender's Association Substantive Law Conference 1999, quoted in *WPA Focus on Women and Justice Newsletter*, October 2003, 2.
17. Ehrenreich and Fox Piven, 37.
18. Goswami and Schervish, 1.
19. Goswami and Schervish, 2.
20. "Barriers to Re-entry," *WPA Focus on Women and Justice Newsletter*, October 2003, 3.
21. Patricia O'Brien, Beyond Media Women in Prison Panel, Chicago, March 25, 2004.
22. "Barriers to Re-entry," *WPA Focus on Women and Justice Newsletter*, October 2003, 1–3.
23. Marion Wright Edelman, *The Measure of Our Success: A Letter to My Children and Yours* (New York: HarperPerennial, 1993), 92.
24. Edelman and Fox Piven, 31.
25. Ibid., n. 22.
26. "Barriers to Re-entry," *WPA Focus on Women and Justice Newsletter*, October 2003, 1–3, 26; Correctional Association of New York, "The Effects of Imprisonment on Families," Women in Prison Project Fact Sheet (New York: Correctional Association of New York, 2002), 2.
27. Correctional Association of New York, "Women Prisoners and Substance Abuse Fact Sheet," Women in Prison Project Fact Sheet (New York: Correctional Association of New York, March 2002), 1.
28. Amnesty International, "Rights for All: Violations of Human Rights for Women," AIUSA Fact Sheet (Washington, D.C.: Amnesty International Publications, 1998), 2.
29. Susan George and Robert LaLonde, "Incarcerated Mothers: The Chicago Project on Female Prisoners and Their Children," University of Chicago Irving B. Harris Graduate School of Public Policy Report to Congressional Black Caucasus, September 14, 2002, 3–5.

CHAPTER 12

1. Wenona Thompson, "I Hate Not Having Control," unpublished poem.
2. Wenona Thompson, interview with the author, June 2004.
3. Wenona Thompson, "The Day My Mother Was Sent Away," unpublished poem.
4. Thompson interview.
5. Joy James, *Resisting State Violence: Radicalism, Gender and Race in U.S. Culture* (Minneapolis: University of Minnesota Press, 1996), 151.
6. Thompson interview.
7. Thompson interview.
8. James, 148.
9. Thompson interview.
10. Wenona Thompson, panelist at Beyond Media's Women in Prison Panel, March 25, 2004.
11. Thompson interview.
12. Nancy Campbell, *Using Women: Gender, Drug Policy, and Social Justice* (New York: Routledge, 2000), 222.
13. Thompson interview.
14. Thompson interview.
15. Thompson interview.
16. Meghan Scahill, "Female Delinquency Cases 1997," Office of Juvenile Justice and Delinquency Prevention Fact Sheet (Washington, D.C.: U.S. Government Printing Office, 2000), 1.
17. Leslie Acoca, "Investing in Girls: A 21st Century Strategy," *Journal of the Office of Juvenile Justice and Delinquency Prevention*, VI, no. 1 (1999): 6.
18. Acoca, 6.
19. Acoca, 8.
20. Elizabeth Cauffman and Shirley Feldman, "Posttraumatic Stress Disorder among Female Juvenile Offenders," *Journal of the American Academy of Child and Adolescent Psychiatry*, no. 37 (1998): 1209–16.
21. Nora Acosta, interview with the author, Las Lunas, New Mexico, March 2002.
22. Acosta interview.
23. Acosta interview.
24. Acosta interview.
25. Acosta interview.
26. Angie Vachio, interview with the author, March 2002.
27. Katherine Gabel and Denise Johnston, *Children of Incarcerated Parents* (New York: Lexington Books, 1995), 199–232.
28. Martha Aragon, interview with the author, New Mexico, March 2002.
29. Aragon interview.
30. Aragon interview.
31. Aragon interview.
32. Aragon interview.

INDEX